PREFACE

The questions in this book are intended to provide a source of new material for classroom use, homework and revision for GCSE. They have been arranged from easier (standard) to more difficult (extension), without attempting to categorise each individual question. A more prescriptive description would be of limited value due to the different demands of specific syllabuses.

Objective and structured questions testing biological knowledge and biological processes have been arranged within major themes common to all syllabuses. The number of questions contained in each of these themes reflects the approximate mark value indicated by the various examining groups.

With much novel material being included, we hope teachers and pupils will find this book both challenging and useful.

☐ Elza Margrain ☐ Alan Robinson
☐ Bob Margrain ☐ John Stevenson
     Dalriada School, Ballymoney

CONTENTS

Theme 1   Diversity   1

Theme 2   Inter-relationships   16

Ecology
Questions 1–11:   Food chains and food webs
Questions 12–20:   Cycles of matter
Questions 21–25:   Soil
Questions 26–35:   Populations
Questions 36–54:   Man's impact on nature

Micro-organisms
Questions 55–63:   General microbiology
Questions 64–73:   Food production and preservation
Questions 74–90:   Microbes and disease

Theme 3   Maintenance and organisation   58
Questions 1–10:   Cells
Questions 11–23:   Enzymes
Questions 24–38:   Osmoregulation and the kidney
Questions 39–57:   Plant nutrition and structure
Questions 58–74:   Animal nutrition and diet
Questions 75–85:   Transport in plants
Questions 86–101:   Transport in animals
Questions 102–120:   Respiration and gas exchange
Questions 121–124:   Sensitivity in plants
Questions 125–133:   Receptors
Questions 134–141:   Nervous system
Questions 142–150:   Effectors
Questions 151–156:   Hormones

G·C·S·E
BIOLOGY
Q·U·E·S·T·I·O·N·S

E Margrain · R Margrain · A Robinson · J Stevenson

Blackie

G·C·S·E BIOLOGY Q·U·E·S·T·I·O·N·S

ISBN 0 216 92416 2

First published 1988

© Elza Margrain, Bob Margrain, Alan Robinson
and John Stevenson 1988

Illustrated by the authors

Published by Blackie and Son Ltd
Bishopbriggs, Glasgow G64 2NZ
7 Leicester Place, London WC2H 7BP

British Library Cataloguing in Publication Data

GCSE biology questions
    1. Organisms — Questions & answers —
For schools
I. Margrain, Elza
574'.076

   ISBN 0–216–92416–2

Filmset by Advanced Filmsetters (Glasgow) Ltd
Printed and bound by Bell and Bain Ltd, Glasgow

Theme 4   Development and continuity of life   132

Cell division
Questions 1–8:   Normal cell division
Questions 9–13:   Cancer cells

Reproduction
Questions 14–23:   Plant reproduction
Questions 24–32:   Animal reproduction

Development
Questions 33–43:   Plant development
Questions 44–51:   Animal development
Questions 52–64:   Inheritance
Questions 65–74:   Selection

Answers   163

Theme 1
Diversity

MULTIPLE CHOICE QUESTIONS

1   In the field of biology, the major distinction between organisms which are called *animals* and organisms which are called *plants* is made on the basis of the organism's type of:

A   respiration   B   locomotion   C   excretion
D   nutrition   E   reproduction

2   Which one of the following is **not** a characteristic of living organisms?

A   excretion
B   respiration
C   expansion
D   sensitivity
E   movement

3   Living organisms have a number of characteristics in common. Which one of the following is a correct list of characteristics which would be true of any living organism?

A   respiration; excretion; hearing
B   excretion; reproduction; respiration
C   reproduction; growth; photosynthesis
D   sight; excretion; growth
E   breathing; reproduction; excretion

4   Which one of the following is **not** a characteristic of insects?

A   they have four pairs of legs
B   they have a hard, outside skeleton
C   they have compound eyes
D   their body is divided into three parts
E   they may have wings

5   If an animal lives in the sea, breathes air and lays its eggs on land, it is probably:

A   a mammal
B   an amphibian
C   a reptile
D   a fish
E   a vertebrate

1

6 A bat is a mammal because:

A it can fly
B it can move about in the dark
C it is warm-blooded
D it has fur
E it feeds on insects

7 If an organism does not contain chlorophyll, is composed of many cells and reproduces with spores, it is probably a:

A fern   B protozoan   C plant   D moss   E fungus

8 Which one of the following pairs correctly shows a plant group and one of its major characteristics?

A algae——roots
B flowering plants——spores
C fungi——no chlorophyll
D ferns——flowers
E mosses——seeds

EXTENSION QUESTION

9 The following is a list of the characteristics of some organisms.

> spores; hard outside skeleton; stems and roots; may have wings; contain chlorophyll; body divided into three parts

Which one of the following pairs of groups of organisms have all of the above characteristics between them?

A insects and ferns ˴
B jellyfish and algae
C crustaceans and flowering plants
D round worms and mosses
E true worms and conifers

STRUCTURED QUESTIONS

10 Invertebrates are animals without an inside skeleton made of bone. There are many groups of invertebrates. Here is a key for the identification of 8 common groups of them.

1 The animal has jointed legs .... Yes   go to **2**
.........No   go to **3**

2 The animal has at least
4 pairs of jointed legs............... Yes   go to **4**
.... No   **insects**

2

3	The animal has a shell	Yes	**molluscs**
		No	go to **5**
4	The animal lives in the sea	Yes	**crustaceans**
		No	**spiders**
5	The animal has stinging tentacles	Yes	**coelenterates**
		No	go to **6**
6	The animal's body is divided into many segments	Yes	**annelids**
		No	go to **7**
7	The animal has five arms	Yes	**starfish**
		No	**flatworms**

(a) Now use this key to place 8 of the following animals in their correct group.

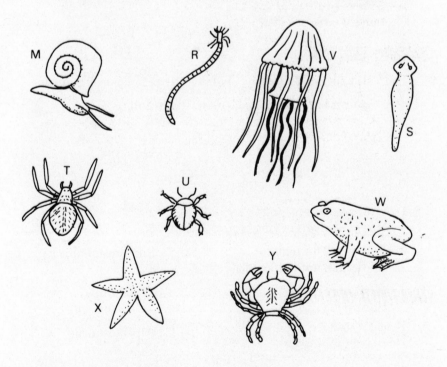

(b) Which animal is left over?
(c) Why does it not belong to any of the 8 groups?

11 Examine the diagrams of dinosaurs and then identify them using the key which follows.

1   Over six metres long 2
     Under six metres long 5

2   End of tail flattened.................... **Euoplocephalus**
     End of tail not flattened............... 3

3   Has horns .... **Triceratops**
     Has no horns 4

4   Has a large head .... **Albertosaurus**
     Has a small head .... **Apatosaurus**

5   Two metres in length 6
     Three metres in length .... **Scelidosaurus**

6   Walks on two legs .... **Stenonchosaurus**
     Walks on four legs..................... **Psittacosaurus**

12 Examine the following diagrams of six species of insect which live in fresh water.

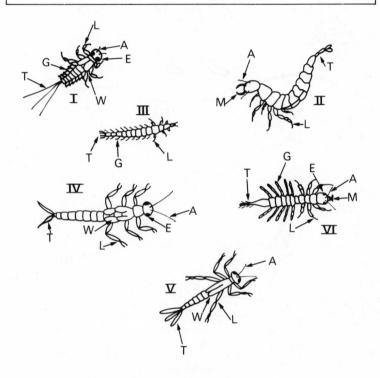

Key: A = antenna T = tail filament E = eye L = leg
G = gill W = wing bud M = mouth

Using the key below, identify the six insects.

1 Animal with gills along its body **2**
Animal with no gills along its body . . **4**

2 Animal with one tail filament . . . . **alder fly nymph**
Animal with more than one tail
filament **3**

3 Gills like small leaves . . . . **mayfly nymph**
Gills like fine hairs . . . . **whirligig beetle
larva**

4 Animal without wing buds . . . . **great diving
beetle larva**

Animal with wing buds **5**

5 Animal with two tail filaments . . . . **stone fly nymph**
Animal with three tail filaments . . . . . . **damsel fly nymph**

5

13 Examine the following diagrams of different leaves and then identify them using the key below.

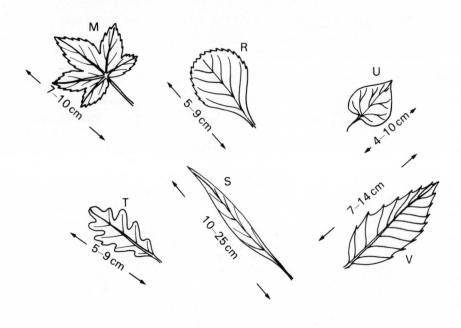

1 Leaf lobed **2**
Leaf not lobed **3**

2 Lobes pointed and leaf edge serrated.... **sycamore**
Lobes rounded and leaf edge not
serrated.................................. **oak**

3 Leaf at least twice as long as broad...... **4**
Leaf not twice as long as broad.......... **5**

4 Leaf with smooth edge .... **willow**
Leaf with toothed edge.................. **sweet chestnut**

5 Leaf pointed at the end.................. **lilac**
Leaf not pointed at the end .... **alder**

14 Examine the following diagrams of six species of fungi.

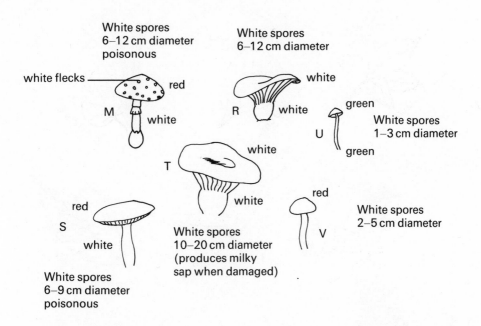

White spores
6–12 cm diameter
poisonous

white flecks

red

M

white

White spores
6–12 cm diameter

white

R

white

green

U

green

White spores
1–3 cm diameter

white

T

white

red

white

S

red

V

White spores
2–5 cm diameter

white

White spores
10–20 cm diameter
(produces milky
sap when damaged)

White spores
6–9 cm diameter
poisonous

(a) Use the key to identify each species.
1 Red..................................2
Not red..............................4

2 Red cap with white flecks............**scarlet flycap**
Pure red cap **3**

3 Cap less than 6 cm across............**scarlet wax cap**
Cap more than 6 cm across..........**sickener**

4 White................................**5**
Green ....**parrot wax cap**

5 Produces milky sap when damaged . **fleecy milk cap**
Does not produce milky sap when
damaged.............................**milk white russula**

(b) What characteristic of these species could **not** have been used
in making a key?
(c) Explain your answer to **(b)**.
(d) Give one other characteristic which could have been used to
separate the sickener from the scarlet wax cap.

15 Examine the drawings of animals and plants.

Copy out the following table and fill in the blanks. The first line has been completed for you.

Group	Code letter	Characteristic
Mammals	B	Body covered with fur
	I	
Algae		
Molluscs		
		Plants with flowers
Birds		
	L	
Ferns		
	G	
		Scales; fins
Mosses		
	C	
	D	

16 The following three animals can be found on the seashore.

(a) To what phylum do they belong?
(b) Give two characteristics which they all have.
(c) What characteristic of this phylum does not **appear** to be shared by all three?
(d) Why is this?

17 Look at the following pictures, which all show animals belonging to the group known as *arthropods*.

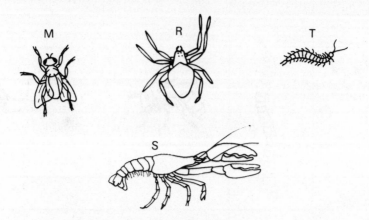

(a) In which animal(s) is the body divided into:
   (i) three distinct parts?
   (ii) more than three distinct parts?
   (iii) two distinct parts?
(b) In which animal(s) are there:
   (i) two pairs of legs?
   (ii) three pairs of legs?
   (iii) four pairs of legs?
   (iv) more than four pairs of legs?
(c) Which animal(s) have feelers?
(d) Which animal has wings?
(e) Which animal has legs modified into claws?
(f) Give two differences between spiders and insects.
(g) Give two common characteristics common to all arthropods.
(h) Identify the following groups by their letters.
   (i) spiders
   (ii) crustaceans
   (iii) insects
   (iv) myriapods

18 Examine the following simplified diagrams of animals. All these animals are typical of their groups. Now answer the questions by reference to the letters only. *Note: there may be more than one answer to each question.*

(a) Which of the above has a body made of one cell only?

(b) Which can breathe oxygen dissolved in water?

(c) Which can possess male and female reproductive organs in the same individual?

(d) Which are warm-blooded?

(e) Which are invertebrates?

(f) Which vertebrates produce eggs in waterproof coats?

(g) Which have lungs?

(h) Which one belongs to the commonest class of animals?

(i) Which undergo metamorphosis?

(j) Which one has a single, muscular foot?

19 The following diagram shows an insect (a beetle) which is found in leaf litter. Examine the diagram carefully and then answer the questions.

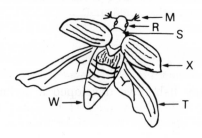

(a) Name the structures M, R, S, T and W.
(b) What are the functions of:
   (i) M?
   (ii) R?
(c) This insect has two pairs of wings but only the hind pair are used for flight. The fore wings have become toughened and, when folded, they cover the hind wings. Why is this necessary?
(d) Give two characteristics of the organism which identify it as an insect.

20 The *birds* are a class of vertebrates usually described as being warm-blooded and feathered, with forelimbs developed into wings. They reproduce by laying eggs.

(a) Give one other characteristic which birds share with all other vertebrates, and which is not mentioned above.
(b) How do birds manage to eat hard foodstuffs such as seeds and nuts when they do not possess teeth?
(c) Which other vertebrate class is usually described as being 'warm-blooded'?
(d) Which other vertebrate classes generally lay eggs?
(e) Name a vertebrate that is **not** a bird but which also has its forelimbs developed into wings.
(f) Give two functions of bird feathers.

21 (a) Give two characteristics of fish.
(b) Are fish cold-blooded or warm-blooded?
(c) Read the following passage carefully and then answer the questions below. You may need to use your own biological knowledge as well as the information given in the passage in order to answer the questions.

'Fish may be divided into two groups: those with a skeleton of cartilage and those with a skeleton of bone. Bony fish have developed a swim bladder which provides buoyancy. This allows the front fins to be used for very refined swimming movements instead of providing lift, as they do in cartilaginous fish. These refined movements allow bony fish to stop and to swim backwards.

Fish are sensitive to sound and light. Bony fish have rods and cones in the retinas of their eyes, whereas cartilaginous fish have only rods.

In tropical lakes and rivers and around coral reefs, feeding is particularly good. Large numbers of species of bony fish live in close proximity and here, bright colours aid in species identification.'

(i) What structure helps to keep cartilaginous fish from sinking?
(ii) What structure helps to keep bony fish afloat?
(iii) What extra abilities does the structure in (ii) give bony fish?
(iv) Why would it be a waste of time for cartilaginous fish to be brightly coloured?
(v) Why are there large numbers of fish living in and around coral reefs?
(vi) Give one reason why bony fish living around coral reefs need to be brightly coloured.

22 (a) What is the one essential difference between a plant and an animal?

(b) What differences would there be between a typical plant cell, e.g. a mesophyll cell of a leaf of a flowering plant, and a typical animal cell, e.g. a human cheek cell?

(c) Read the following passage carefully, then try to answer the questions below.

> 'Plants are found growing all over the Earth, in cold places and in hot places, in dry places and in wet places. A number of different groups of plants are recognised by biologists. The *algae* are usually regarded as the simplest plants: they always contain the green pigment, chlorophyll, and several other pigments as well. The *bryophytes* are small plants that live in moist places; they contain chlorophyll and reproduce by spores. The *pteridophytes* are also green and reproduce by spores, but they are much larger plants and they contain vascular tissue. The *spermatophytes* include the flowering plants. Most species of plant fall into this group—these plants are very diverse and can reproduce by the production of seeds and fruits.'

(i) To which of the groups mentioned in the passage would a common seaweed belong?

(ii) Give one example of a bryophyte.

(iii) Give one example of a pteridophyte.

(iv) Why can pteridophytes grow taller than bryophytes?

(v) Which of the groups mentioned is best adapted to life on land?

23 The following diagram illustrates a section through an earthworm. The characteristics of earthworms are as follows:

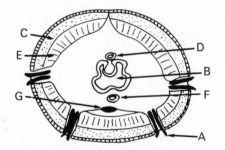

dorsal and ventral blood vessels
solid ventral nerve cord
central digestive system
two layers of muscles
pairs of chaetae (bristles)

Using the above information, name the structures labelled A–G on the diagram.

24 Read the following information about plants.

> The plant kingdom can be separated into five divisions: algae, fungi, mosses, ferns and seed-bearing plants.
>
> There are two major groups of seed-bearing plants: flowering plants and conifers. Conifers bear cones from which winged seeds are released. Seaweeds belong to the algae and they contain, as well as chlorophyll, other photosynthetic pigments, so that some seaweeds are red or brown.
>
> Fungi are the only group which do not possess any photosynthetic pigments, although they, too, can be green, red and brown. Some of the most poisonous fungi are brightly coloured, however the lethal Death Cap is an exception: it is pure white. Mosses have no transporting tissue in their bodies, but they can absorb water through their entire surface when moisture is available.
>
> Fungi, mosses and ferns all reproduce by small, light spores. In ferns, these spores are produced on the lower surface of green fronds.

Use the following key to say whether the statements given below are:

A *supported by the above information*
B *contradicted by the above information*
C *neither supported nor contradicted by the above information*

(a) All seaweeds require light to manufacture their own food.
(b) Coloured fungi can photosynthesise.
(c) Conifers are wind-pollinated.
(d) Mosses are entirely restricted to damp habitats.
(e) Spores of fungi, mosses and ferns are wind-dispersed.
(f) All poisonous fungi are brightly coloured.
(g) Mosses have roots with identical functions to those of flowering plants.
(h) All conifers are trees.
(i) Seeds of conifers are wind-dispersed.
(j) Flowering plants are the most highly adapted group of plants.
(k) The fronds of ferns have both reproductive and photosynthetic functions.

Theme 2
Inter-relationships

MULTIPLE CHOICE QUESTIONS

1 Which one of the following food chains is correct?

    A   herbivores⟶carnivores⟶carnivores

    B   producers⟶carnivores⟶carnivores

    C   plants⟶secondary consumers⟶tertiary consumers

    D   producers⟶primary consumers⟶secondary consumers

    E   producers⟶secondary consumers⟶tertiary consumers

2 Which one of the following food chains includes a parasite/host relationship?

    A   grass⟶rabbit⟶fox

    B   phytoplankton⟶zooplankton⟶herring

    C   grass⟶grasshoppers⟶frogs

    D   acorns⟶mice⟶owls

    E   grass⟶sheep⟶tick

3 The total amount of energy entering a trophic level is always less than the amount passed on to the next trophic level because:

    A   not all the energy from sunlight is absorbed by plants

    B   energy is needed for the evaporation of water

    C   each trophic level loses energy in respiration

    D   decomposers always use energy

    E   not all herbivores are eaten by predators

EXTENSION QUESTION

4 Which one of the following pairs of food chains corresponds to the two pyramids of numbers below?

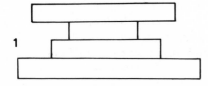 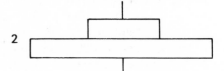

A   **1** phytoplankton⟶water fleas⟶roach⟶pike
    2 algae⟶flatworms⟶waterboatmen⟶great diving
                                       beetle
B   **1** dead leaves⟶worms⟶thrushes⟶fleas
    2 oak tree⟶caterpillars⟶thrushes⟶owl
C   **1** grass⟶elephant⟶ticks⟶tick bird
    2 phytoplankton⟶water fleas⟶herring⟶whale
D   **1** grass⟶grasshoppers⟶frogs⟶stoat
    2 sycamore tree⟶greenfly⟶ladybird⟶blackbird
E   **1** phytoplankton⟶water fleas⟶shrimps⟶herring
    2 cactus⟶maggots⟶small birds⟶hawk

STRUCTURED QUESTIONS

5   Examine the following diagram of a food web.

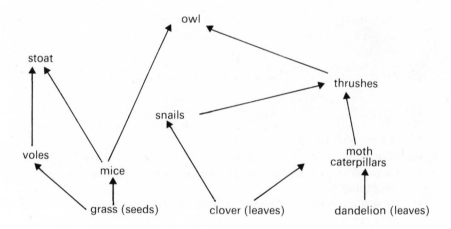

(a) Draw a food chain involving *four* organisms from the web
    given above. Indicate which is the producer, primary consumer,
    secondary consumer and tertiary consumer.
(b) From the food web:
   (i) name another producer;
  (ii) name another primary consumer;
 (iii) name another secondary consumer.
(c) Give one possible connection which is *not* made in the food
    web as it is drawn.

6 The following diagram shows part of a food web in a pond.

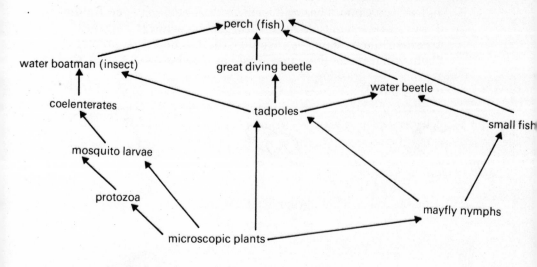

(a) From the above, write out the food chain which has the greatest number of steps in it.

(b) Which organisms are primary consumers *only*?

(c) Which organisms are primary *and* secondary consumers?

(d) Which organisms are omnivores?

(e) Which organisms are carnivores?

(f) How many groups (phyla) of invertebrates are shown in this food web?

(g) How many groups (classes) of vertebrates are shown, and what are they?

7 (a) The lines below show the relative sizes of some pond organisms.

| diatom (plant) | water boatman | water mite | water flea | mayfly nymph |

Herbivores are animals which feed on plants.

Carnivores are animals which feed on other animals.

Larger carnivores feed on smaller carnivores.

Using the above information, construct a chain to show which of the above organisms feed on which.

(b) The following diagrams show some fresh water organisms, and also an aquarium. The organisms are not drawn to scale. Study them carefully and then draw out a table to show the areas of the aquarium in which you would expect to find these animals. There will be more than one animal in some areas.

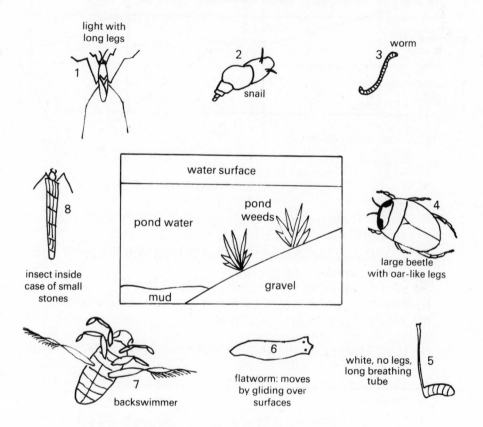

8 The following is a list of some of the organisms found in an oak wood. Those underlined feed on other animals.

oak trees   heather   slugs   <u>hedgehogs</u>   <u>blackbirds</u>   fungi
dung beetles   <u>foxes</u>   bees   brambles   <u>thrush</u>   mice   nettles

(a) Name the producers in this system.
(b) Name three primary consumers.
(c) Draw out two food chains, using different organisms from the list above.
(d) Which organisms in the list are saprophytes?
(e) What is their function in such a community?
(f) What is the function of the dung beetles?

9 Examine the table below and then answer the questions which follow.

	Fate of food		
Animal	%not digested	% used for growth	% used for respiration
Herbivore e.g. cow	60	x	30
Carnivore e.g. lion	20	y	70

(a) What is the value of:
  (i) x?
  (ii) y?
(b) What total percentage of the herbivore's food is digested and used?
(c) Why is this percentage smaller than the value for the carnivore?
(d) If a cow eats 1000 kg of hay, how much of this is converted into beef?
(e) If a lion eats 500 kg of zebra, how much of this will be used for growth?

10 The information tabulated below was collected from the intertidal zone of a rocky sea shore.

Name of organism	Density/m²	Wet weight of one individual/g
Bladder wrack	20	150
Knotted wrack	40	200
Serrated wrack	20	100
Limpet	60	10
Periwinkle	20	5
Starfish	1	50

The wracks are seaweeds.
Limpets and periwinkles are herbivores.
Starfish are carnivores.

(a) Use the information given to construct a pyramid of numbers.
(b) Use the wet weight information and the density to construct a pyramid of biomass (use units of g/m²).
(c) In what way is a pyramid of biomass preferable to a pyramid of numbers?
(d) It is preferable to use dry weight rather than wet weight when constructing a pyramid of biomass. Briefly explain why this is so.
(e) Describe how you would determine the dry weight of a seaweed, such as bladder wrack.

11 Examine the following diagram and then answer the questions using the key provided.

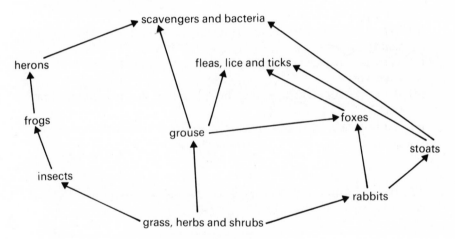

Key: **A** *supported by the diagram*
B *contradicted by the diagram*
C *neither supported nor contradicted by the diagram*

(a) In this food web, insects are producers.
(b) Herons feed on material which comes indirectly from herbs and shrubs.
(c) The greatest amount of food energy is consumed by the scavengers and bacteria.
(d) Stoats are herbivores.
(e) The scavengers and bacteria help reduce organic material.
(f) If more grouse than usual are shot during a particular season, the number of other primary consumers would decrease.
(g) Herons are herbivores.
(h) Fleas are secondary and tertiary consumers.

12 The major reservoir of the element nitrogen, which is vital to plant and animal growth, is to be found:

A   in soil
B   in air
C   in plants
D   in animals
E   in decomposers

13 In which one of the following is oxygen **not** involved?

A   combustion   B   decomposition   C   respiration
D   fermentation   E   photosynthesis

14 The diagram below shows a simplified water cycle involving a tree.

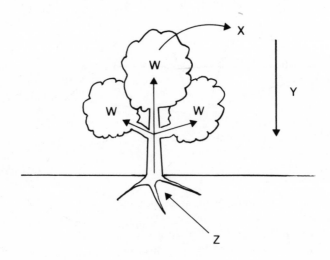

Which one of the following best describes this?

| W | X | Y | Z |

A   transpiration, precipitation, evaporation, absorption
B   translocation, transpiration, precipitation, absorption
C   water transport, transpiration, rainfall, osmotic uptake
D   water transport, transpiration, precipitation, active uptake
E   water transport, evaporation, translocation, absorption

EXTENSION QUESTION

15 Which one of the following is **not** part of the carbon cycle?
(The arrows indicate the direction of flow.)

A   animal respiration⟶carbon dioxide⟶photosynthesis
B   photosynthesis⟶complex carbon compounds⟶animal
                                                                                nutrition
C   animal respiration⟶carbon dioxide⟵plant respiration
D   decomposers⟶carbon dioxide⟶photosynthesis
E   animal nutrition⟵complex carbon compounds⟶photo-
                                                                                synthesis

STRUCTURED QUESTIONS

16 Examine the diagram below, which represents the nitrogen cycle.

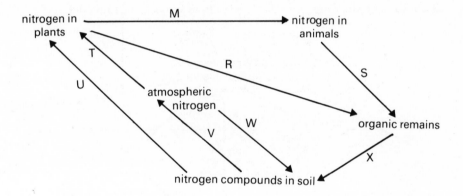

(a) Which letters indicate the process of nitrogen fixation?
(b) Which letters indicate the processes of death or defaecation?
(c) What is indicated by the letter M?
(d) What is indicated by the letter U?
(e) What is indicated by the letter X?
(f) What is indicated by the letter V?

17 A farm may be thought of as an ecosystem. Some of the components of a farm ecosystem are listed below.

outbuildings	fertiliser
manure heap	hens
cattle	farm dog
bales of hay	grain
pasture	farmer

(a) Which of the above makes organic compounds from simple, inorganic compounds?

(b) In what forms are these organic compounds stored on the farm before they are consumed?

(c) Which animals may benefit first from this stored food?

(d) Where may the organic compounds be broken down into ammonia and nitrates?

(e) Give two sources of nitrogen on the farm.

(f) Give two primary consumers on the farm.

(g) Give two secondary consumers on the farm.

(h) By what process is organic carbon lost from this ecosystem?

(i) How does energy enter the farm ecosystem?

18 Examine the diagram below, which shows the carbon cycle.

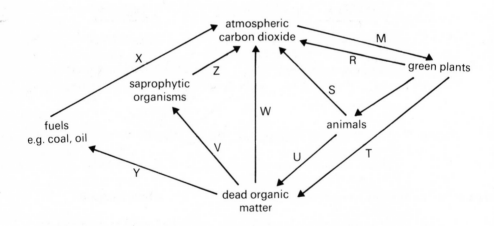

(a) What important processes are occurring at M, R, S, X and Z?

(b) Give two ways in which T and U can occur.

(c) Under what special conditions will Y occur?

(d) What name would you give to V and what sort of saprophytic organisms are responsible for the change?

(e) How could W occur naturally, and what does man do which assists this process?

(f) Why don't M and R cancel each other out?

19 The recycling of materials is important in the biosphere. Nitrogen is recycled by means of decomposers within the soil.
Given the following information, construct as complete a nitrogen cycle as possible.

1 Plants are eaten by animals.
2 Plants can only take up nitrogen, as nitrates, through their roots.
3 When plants and animals die, bacteria in the soil break their protein down into ammonia.
4 In the breakdown process, ammonia is converted into nitrites, which are then converted to nitrates.
5 *Nitrobacter* is a bacterium which converts nitrites to nitrates.
6 *Nitrosomonas* is a bacterium which converts ammonia to nitrites.
7 *Azotobacter* is a bacterium which lives in the soil and converts atmospheric nitrogen to nitrates.

EXTENSION QUESTION

20 Below are shown two possible methods for treating sewage and making use of the end products.

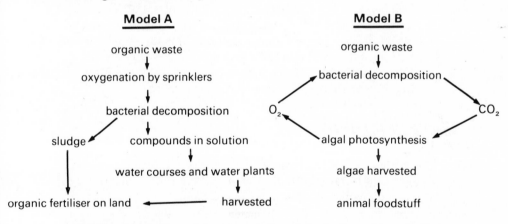

(a) What kind of useful compounds might be found in solution or in the sludge in Model A?
(b) Why are these compounds useful as fertilisers?
(c) Model B is a proposed method of dealing with sewage in *warmer* climates than our own. Why might such a system not work in Britain?
(d) Give one problem that would have to be overcome in order to harvest the algae.
(e) What could be added to Model B to make it an example of a simple nitrogen cycle?

MULTIPLE CHOICE QUESTIONS

21 Sandy soils characteristically have:

   A   large particles, large air spaces, few minerals
   B   large particles, small air spaces, abundant minerals
   C   small particles, abundant oxygen, few minerals
   D   small particles, good crumb structure, many organisms
   E   large particles, abundant oxygen, abundant water

EXTENSION QUESTION

22 Which of the following gives the **best** description of soil?

   A   Soil is made up of organic and inorganic particles, between which there is the soil atmosphere and soil water. All of this provides a suitable habitat for a large variety of microscopic organisms.
   B   Soil is made up of large and small particles, between which there is air and water.
   C   Soil is made up of a mixture of particles, between which a large variety of soil organisms live because the spaces between the particles allow oxygen and water to be present.
   D   Soil is made up of living and non-living material. The non-living part of it consists of sand and clay, with air and water in the spaces. The living material is the soil organisms.
   E   Soil is made up of inorganic particles of a range of sizes. Between these particles, humus, air and water are found, together with a wide range of soil organisms.

STRUCTURED QUESTIONS

23 Three soil samples, A, B and C, from different locations, were analysed for humus content, water content and permeability to water. The results are given in the table below.

	A	B	C
Humus content (% by weight of wet soil)	4	5	20
Water content (% by weight)	10	50	20
Permeability to water (g of water passing through 100 g soil in 1 minute)	45	6	25

(a) Which one of these soils would be best for plant growth?

(b) Give one reason for your answer to **(a)**.

(c) Why is the air content of the soil necessary for plant growth?

(d) One of these soils is described as 'a very light, sandy soil'. Which one?

(e) Give one reason for your answer to **(d)**.

(f) Why is the humus content of the soil important?

24 Look carefully at this diagram of a piece of biological apparatus and then answer the questions which follow.

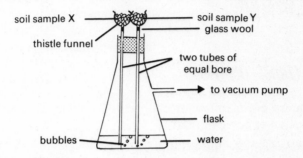

(a) When the vacuum pump is switched on, bubbles appear in the water, coming from the two tubes. (This is shown happening on the diagram.)

   (i) What are these bubbles?

   (ii) Explain where the bubbles have come from.

   (iii) Why is it important that the two long, vertical tubes are of equal internal diameter?

   (iv) Where in this apparatus would you expect to have airtight seals?

(b) In an experiment, samples of soil were taken from two different locations and placed in the thistle funnels of the above apparatus. An equal volume of freshly dug soil was placed in each. The vacuum pump was turned on and the numbers of bubbles appearing in the water were counted for one minute. The results are given below.

	From sample X	From sample Y
Number of bubbles per minute	16	42

   (i) What property of soil is being measured by this apparatus?

   (ii) Why is it important that fresh soil is used?

   (iii) Why is it important that equal volumes of soil are used?

   (iv) Suggest possible sources for the two soil samples, X and Y.

25 In the Ethiopian highlands, it has been common practice to cut
    down trees for food, fuel and building materials. Now it appears
    that the production of crops in the area is being severely hampered
    by the disappearance of the topsoil in vast quantities.

    (a) How do you think deforestation leads to soil erosion?
    (b) Why is this a particular problem in mountainous regions?
    (c) How does soil loss reduce the amount of the harvest?
    (d) Can you make two practical suggestions of steps that could be
    taken to conserve the remaining topsoil in this area?

MULTIPLE CHOICE QUESTIONS

26 Which one of the following could cause an increase in a
    population of green plants?

    A   increase in available light
    B   decrease in available water
    C   decrease in space available
    D   increase in the number of herbivores
    E   increase in disease

27 In lowland farms, sheep may be grazed at a density of 10 per
    hectare; however in upland areas, the stocking density of sheep is
    usually 1 per hectare. This lower stocking density is due to:

    A   competition with cattle
    B   the slow growth of vegetation
    C   overcrowding, which causes the spread of disease
    D   a requirement for plenty of space for exercise
    E   the numbers being kept down by predators

EXTENSION QUESTION

28 When will a rabbit population **not** increase in numbers?

    A   when the birth rate exceeds the mortality rate
    B   when the number eaten by foxes is less than the number being
        born
    C   when the immigration rate is the same as the birth rate
    D   when the immigration rate is higher than the mortality rate
    E   when the emigration rate exceeds the birth rate

29 The following map shows the area in which a group of biologists
collected earthworms using formalin sprinkled on a 1 m² quadrat.
Five quadrat samples were taken from different parts of the area.
The location of each quadrat is marked on the map.

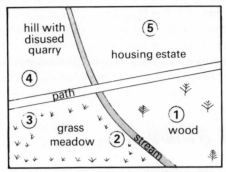

1–5 mark the positions of the quadrats

This table gives the results of the investigation.

Quadrat	Number of worms collected
1	46
2	54
3	28
4	9
5	13
Total	

Now answer the following questions.

(a) What was the total number of worms collected?

(b) What is the average number of worms collected per quadrat?

(c) Given that the total area of the grass meadow is 400 m², use
the two quadrat samples taken from that area to work out an
estimate of the total number of worms in the grass meadow.
Show your working clearly.

(d) Sample 2 was from near the stream, while sample 3 was from
near the path; they both came from the grass meadow. Suggest
why sample 3 contained fewer worms than sample 2.

(e) Give two different reasons why the number of worms from
quadrat samples 4 and 5 are very small.

(f) Give one reason why you think *all* the numbers in the results
table may be lower than the real number of worms living in
each quadrat.

30 Four children were out for a walk in the countryside on a bright, sunny summer's day. Deborah said that she could hear a lot of grasshoppers but Johnathan said that he could not see any. Louise thought they were hiding in the grass beside her, where there happened to be some shade. David said, 'Maybe they like shade!' They all decided to search the area carefully to see if they could find any, and sure enough, they found six. When they searched another area nearby that was in direct sunlight, they only found two.

(a) From the passage, give two specific biological observations made by the children.
(b) From the passage, give two scientific hypotheses suggested by the children.
(c) Presumably they searched the shaded area to test their ideas; but why do you think they searched the second area?

31 The diagrams below show (i) an early stage in the development of a woodland (after 1 year), and (ii) the final stage in the development of the same woodland (after 50 years).

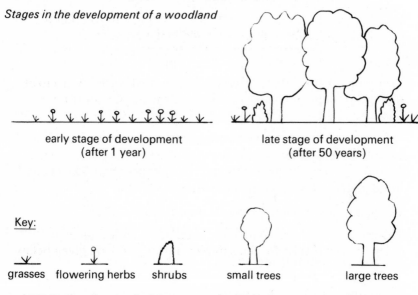

Stages in the development of a woodland

early stage of development
(after 1 year)

late stage of development
(after 50 years)

Key:

grasses flowering herbs shrubs small trees large trees

(a) Using the symbols given in the key, show the developments you would expect to take place after:
  (i) 5 years;
  (ii) 25 years.
(b) What word is used to describe the changes in the plants in such woodland areas over a period of time?
(c) What would you expect to happen to the number and variety of animals present during this period of time?

(d) What term can be used to describe the mature woodland (after 50 years).

(e) Suggest one reason why no plants are growing beneath the trees in the mature woodland.

32 Swallows, house martins and swifts are all migratory birds which spend the summer months in Britain and the winter months in Africa. They all feed on flying insects. Swallows feed nearest the ground, martins higher up and swifts highest of all. Swallows are the first to arrive back in this country in the spring, martins next and swifts arrive back the latest. As air warms up in the spring, it rises, carrying insects to ever higher regions.

(a) What is meant by the term *migratory*?

(b) Why would these three species of birds not find any food in this country in the winter?

(c) Explain why these three species are not in competition with each other for food.

(d) With reference to availability of food, explain why these birds return to this country in the order that they do.

(e) Why is it said to be a sign of forthcoming bad weather if swallows are seen flying just above the grass?

33 Water boatmen are insects which live in freshwater. A group of biology students wished to investigate the number of water boatmen in a pond of area $20 \, m^2$ and depth 1 m.

A large net, with a circular opening of area $0.2 \, m^2$, was used to sample the water boatmen. This was done by sweeping the net steadily through the water for a fixed distance (1 m). The net had therefore sampled a cylinder of water of volume:

$$0.2 \, m^2 \times 1 \, m = 0.2 \, m^3.$$

The number of water boatmen in each net sample was then counted. The results for ten samples of this pond are given below:

$$5 \quad 3 \quad 8 \quad 0 \quad 1 \quad 2 \quad 1 \quad 2 \quad 3 \quad 5$$

(a) Estimate the population of water boatmen in animals per m^3 of pond.

(b) Estimate the total population of water boatmen for the entire pond.

(c) How could you ensure that the net samples in this example were taken at random?

34 Marsh horsetails are plants which live in and around ponds. The number of these plants in a pond of area 20 m² and depth 1 m was under investigation.

Using a quadrat of area 0.25 m², ten samples of the pond surface were taken and the numbers of horsetail plants in each sample were counted. The numbers were:

$$2 \quad 0 \quad 6 \quad 3 \quad 1 \quad 4 \quad 0 \quad 3 \quad 1 \quad 0$$

(a) (i) Calculate the population density of horsetail plants per m².
(ii) Calculate the total number of horsetail plants in the pond.

(b) If you are now told that horsetail plants are rooted and are only found in pond zones where the depth is less than 0.2 m, and that 20% of this pond's area is below this depth, calculate the density of horsetail plants per m² in the horsetail zone.

EXTENSION QUESTION

35 The sycamore aphid (a greenfly or plant bug that feeds on sycamore leaves) lays its eggs in the autumn on the bark of sycamore trees. A branch of a sycamore tree was examined in November using a binocular microscope and the number of aphid eggs was counted on 10 cm sections of the branch. The branch becomes thicker the further one travels from the terminal bud and the bark becomes much rougher. The results of these observations are given below.

Distance of mid-point of section from terminal bud/cm	Number of eggs
5	0
15	0
25	4
35	0
45	0
55	0
65	1
75	0
85	0
95	2
105	2
115	0
125	1
135	18
145	54
155	57
165	76

(a) Why do you think the egg counts were made in November rather than earlier in the autumn, in September?

(b) What was the total number of eggs counted on this branch?

(c) Plot a fully-labelled graph of number of eggs against distance from the terminal bud.

(d) Suggest two explanations for the observation that more eggs appear to be laid at greater distances from the terminal bud.

(e) It has been found that of all the eggs laid in the autumn, only some remain to hatch in the next spring. Suggest two different ways in which eggs might be destroyed during the intervening period.

MULTIPLE CHOICE QUESTIONS

36 Which one of the following is a potential non-polluting source of energy?

  A   oil
  B   natural gas
  C   coal
  D   wind
  E   nuclear fuel

37 When Mount St. Helens exploded in 1980, millions of tonnes of volcanic ash and dust were released into the atmosphere. This covered plants and animals, blocked out the light and drastically altered conditions for many organisms. Although coming from a natural source, the volcanic dust can be regarded as which one of the following:

  A   pesticide
  B   mutagen
  C   carcinogen
  D   mutant
  E   pollutant

38 Which of the following can be described as a non-renewable resource?

  A water   B food   C coal   D fish   E bread

39 Which one of the following would you expect to be the most likely source of a measured increase in radioactivity in the environment?

  A   a leak from a school science laboratory
  B   a leak from a major research laboratory
  C   a leak from an oil-fired power station
  D   a leak from a nuclear power station
  E   a leak from a hydroelectric generating plant

40 Substances that are 'biodegradable' are able to be broken down naturally into simple inorganic substances by the action of bacteria and fungi. This process may take a long time, but 'non-biodegradable' substances cannot be broken down in this way. Which one of the following is a biodegradable waste material?

A   broken wooden chairs
B   broken glass windows
C   iron filings
D   plastic detergent bottles
E   aluminium window frames

41 Which of the following is the best description of the term 'renewable resource'?

A   substances present in infinite quantities in the environment
B   substances used up continually by the environment
C   substances produced by plants
D   substances produced by animals
E   substances that are continually reproduced by natural processes

42 The use of inorganic fertilisers on farmland greatly increases crop production. However, some of the fertiliser can get washed down into streams, rivers and lakes where it can be a pollutant. The damage done by the excess fertiliser in the water is because:

A   the fertiliser is eaten by fish and is poisonous to them
B   the fertiliser eventually causes a lack of oxygen in the water
C   the fertiliser is toxic to water plants
D   the fertiliser deprives the plants of carbon dioxide for photosynthesis
E   the fertiliser causes the temperature of the water to rise

43 Certain chemicals when applied to soil are useful, but if they enter waterways, they are harmful. Select from the list below the two most appropriate terms which describe this.

	Soil	Waterways
A	poisonous	beneficial
B	pollutants	fertilisers
C	enhancing	inhibitory
D	additives	preservatives
E	fertilisers	pollutants

44 Which of the following is **not** necessarily a reason for conservation?

A   maintenance of rare habitats
B   maintenance of a large gene pool
C   ensuring the survival of rare species
D   maintenance of areas as they are today
E   maintenance of species diversity

45 Pesticides are chemicals used to kill species which are regarded as harmful or unwanted in a particular place. Insecticides kill insects, fungicides kill fungi and herbicides kill weeds. Although the use of pesticides can be very beneficial, it can also be a source of pollution. Which one of the following best explains how pesticides can be environmental pollutants?

A   they may get passed on through food chains and harm useful species
B   they may not kill all the pests present
C   organisms may be resistant to the effects of the pesticide
D   each pest may require the application of a different chemical
E   the pesticide may be broken down by organisms in the soil

46 Which one of the following do you think is the major cause of acid rain falling in Scandinavian countries?

A   discharge of acid gases from German power stations
B   discharge of acid gases from domestic sources in Scandinavia
C   discharge of acid gases from industrial sources in Europe
D   discharge of acid gases from car exhausts in Britain
E   discharge of acid gases from the European rail network

EXTENSION QUESTION

47 To *preserve* an ecosystem means to keep it the way that it is.
To *restore* an ecosystem means to put it back to the way it used to be.
The correct relationship between *preservation*, *restoration* and *conservation* is:

A   conservation is always about preservation
B   conservation includes preservation and restoration
C   conservation includes restoration but not preservation
D   preservation includes conservation but not restoration
E   conservation is always about restoration

STRUCTURED QUESTIONS

48 Examine the following world maps which show fishing patterns in 1948 and 1968.

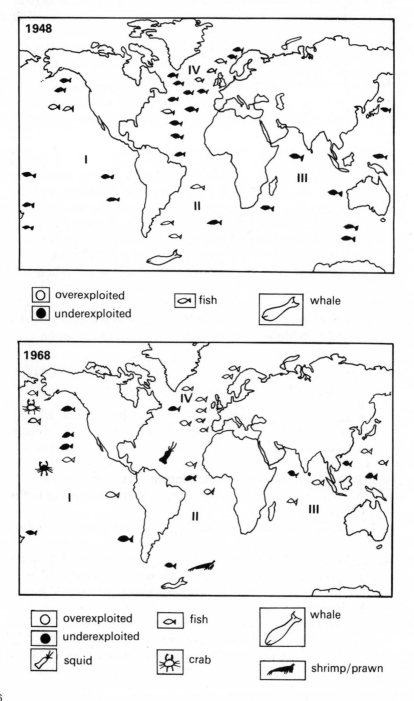

(a) How many species were overexploited in 1948?

(b) How many groups of animals did this include?

(c) How many species of fish were overexploited in 1968?

(d) Which new groups of animals were exploited in 1968?

(e) In which oceans of the world were fish overexploited in 1948?

(f) In which oceans of the world was overexploitation occurring in 1968?

(g) How would the situation in the North Sea and North Atlantic have made life more difficult for British fisherman in 1968?

(h) What species of mammal is overexploited?

49 (a) Puffins are small sea birds that nest in burrows in soft ground on cliffs. They dive underwater for their food. The numbers of puffins around the British coast have been declining, and conservationists are keen to protect the species. Sheep Island, off the coast of Northern Ireland, is a bird sanctuary where there has been a small puffin colony. Several years ago, poison was laid to try to control the increasing rat population.

　(i) In what sense can puffins be described as an endangered species?

　(ii) Why do you think the rats on Sheep Island were killed?

　(iii) Suggest one twentieth century environmental influence that may be contributing to the decline of the puffin population.

(b) Cormorants are large sea birds that also nest on Sheep Island. In the years following the destruction of the rats, the numbers of cormorants increased more than ten times. Recently, cormorants were observed feeding in the River Bush, which flows into the sea not far from Sheep Island. The managers of the salmon station on the Bush have applied for a licence to shoot cormorants on the river.

　(i) Suggest one reason for the increase in cormorants.

　(ii) Why are more cormorants apparently now feeding in the river?

　(iii) Why was it necessary to obtain a licence before shooting cormorants?

(c) Up to two hundred cormorants have been seen feeding along the River Bush in a single day. Each bird can eat up to five young salmon in that time, and the feeding period is about thirty days.

　(i) Calculate the maximum numbers of salmon that could be eaten by the cormorants during the feeding period.

　(ii) In what sense might the cormorants now be regarded as a pest?

50 Examine the following map showing Buffalo ranges in the USA.

map of North America

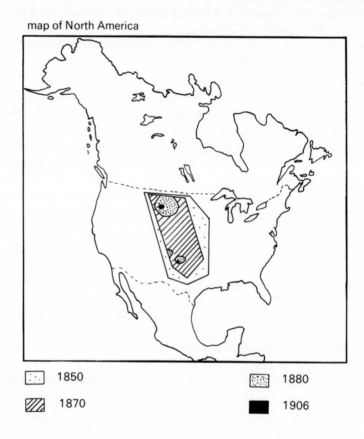

⬚	1850	⬚	1880
▨	1870	⬛	1906

The American Bison (buffalo) was once very numerous. In the early nineteenth century, numbers were estimated at sixty million. The American Indian used the buffalo as the source of all their requirements: food, clothing, tepees, bow strings. They hunted on horseback with bows and arrows.

In the 1860s, the Union Pacific Railway was being built. Teams of professional hunters, including Buffalo Bill, shot the buffalo as food for the construction workers. Between 1870 and 1875, two and a half million animals were killed every year. By 1883, only one herd of ten thousand remained in North Dakota.

(a) Why did the Indian's use of the buffalo not deplete the numbers?

(b) Between which years did the range of the buffalo show its first major decrease?

(c) What was the cause of this?

(d) How many animals were killed from 1870 to 1875 inclusive?

(e) How did Colonel William Cody get his famous nickname?

(f) What reasons, other than food, would the professional hunters have had for killing such large numbers of buffalo?

(g) What effect would this destruction of the buffalo have had on the American Indians?

(h) What is the latest date for which information on buffalo numbers is recorded?

51 In the 1930s there was a small change in the temperature and salinity of the water along a stretch of the Atlantic coast of the USA. A parasitic mould increased in quantity and attacked and destroyed a submerged plant called eelgrass. Almost the entire seashore community of small fish, starfish and worms died out. As well as this, the numbers of a small goose called the brant were reduced to one fifth in the space of a few years. Also, where the eelgrass had disappeared, some of the sandy beaches began to be washed away.

(a) What organisms were dependent on the eelgrass for their survival?

(b) What environmental changes caused the disappearance of the eelgrass?

(c) What organism caused the disappearance of the eelgrass?

(d) Explain why the geese decreased in numbers.

(e) What other job did the eelgrass do, besides being part of a food chain?

(f) What organism benefited from these environmental changes?

52 The rhododendron is an oriental shrub which was introduced to the British Isles from Asia Minor over two hundred years ago. It is a very resilient plant, adapts to lots of different conditions well, and has spread widely and grows wild in many areas. It now forms thick, impenetrable regions in some parts, and grows so densely that very little light penetrates to ground level.

(a) How do you think the spread of the rhododendron has affected the natural shrubs?

(b) What will the ground cover vegetation be like underneath rhododendrons?

(c) What effect will the spread of rhododendrons have on animal populations?

(d) Why, in some locations, is the rhododendron now considered a weed?

(e) How would you go about removing unwanted rhododendrons from an area, bearing in mind the need for conservation of other species.

(f) Do you think it is right to bring new species of plants from one country to another? Explain your answer.

53 Since the beginning of the twentieth century, most of the woodland areas in Northern Ireland have been cleared for building timber, fuel and agriculture. Privately-owned woodlands now only cover 1% of the total land area, 85% of which is farmland. State-owned forests cover 4% of the land, but these are confined to badly-drained, upland areas.

(a) What percentage tree cover is there in N. Ireland?

(b) Why are State-owned forests planted on upland areas only?

(c) Why are State-owned forests almost entirely plantings of conifers, and not deciduous trees?

(d) Why do many conservationists not welcome the planting of conifers on the upland areas of the Province?

Traditionally, trees and hedgerows have provided windbreaks, shelters, renewable timber resources and food for wildlife, but they are now often removed without any consideration being given to their *economic* or *ecological* value. To help counteract this trend, the Department of the Environment and the Department of Agriculture have provided useful advice for farmers. Explain the importance of the advice below in terms of *conservation*.

(e) *The best shape for a hedge is an 'A' shape.*

(f) *Trim the hedges at the* **end** *of the* **winter** *season.*

(g) *Trim farm hedges on a* **rotation** *every third year.*

(h) *Saplings (young trees) growing in hedges should be spared during mechanised hedge-cutting.*

(i) *Artificial fertilisers should not be sprayed into hedge bottoms.*

EXTENSION QUESTION

54 The following diagram illustrates the effect of pollution being added to a river system.

(a) Which organism initially benefits most from the addition of pollutants to the river?

(b) Name four other organisms which benefit at some stage from the addition of pollutants to the river.

(c) Which of the organisms in **(b)** are animals?

(d) Explain the disappearance of the normal algae.

(e) Which animal initially is *most* affected by the pollution?

(f) Explain your answer to **(e)**.

(g) Which of the species mentioned fails to return to its normal level?

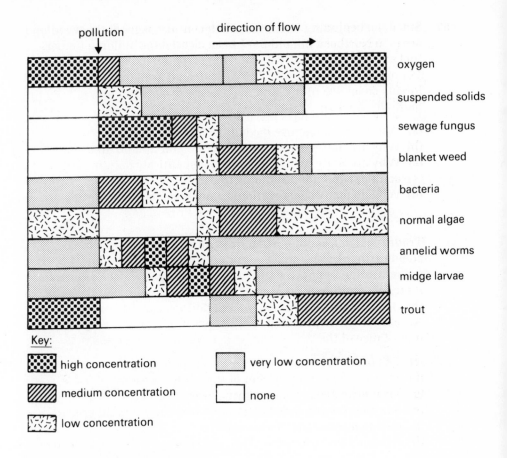

Key:

▓▓ high concentration   ░░ very low concentration

▨▨ medium concentration   ☐ none

▨▨ low concentration

MULTIPLE CHOICE QUESTIONS

55 Which of the following is **not** a microbe?

    A   the virus that causes polio
    B   the algae that grow on the seashore
    C   the amoeba that causes dysentery
    D   the bacterium that causes tuberculosis
    E   the fungus that is used to make bread

56 Which one of the following lists correctly gives these three kinds of microbe in **ascending** order of size?

    A   bacteria, viruses, protozoa
    B   bacteria, protozoa, viruses
    C   protozoa, bacteria, viruses
    D   viruses, bacteria, protozoa
    E   viruses, protozoa, bacteria

57 Microbes were first seen in the seventeenth century by Antonie Van Leeuwenhoek because:

    A   he had remarkable eyesight
    B   he discovered the microscope
    C   he used an electron microscope
    D   this was when they evolved
    E   he invented a microscope with a powerful lens.

EXTENSION QUESTION

58 For bacteria to grow they require:

    A   water, food, a suitable temperature, space
    B   water, light, food, space
    C   light, water, temperatures below 0 °C, space
    D   water, temperatures above 100 °C, space, food
    E   food, light, temperatures above 100 °C, space

STRUCTURED QUESTIONS

59 Look at the diagrams below which show different types of bacteria, then match each bacterium to the correct number from the following key.

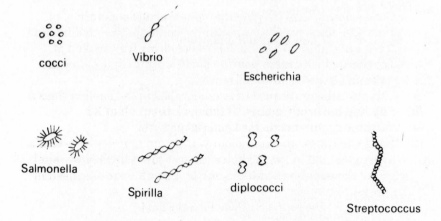

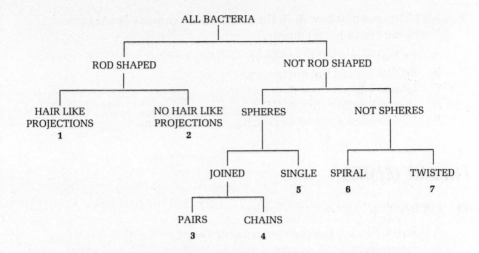

60 Diagram 1 shows a Pasteur flask.

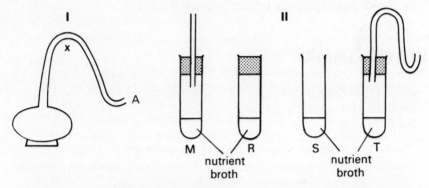

Pasteur used this to investigate the 'spontaneous generation' of microbes. The flask was heated until the contents were boiling and steam issued from A. When the flask cooled, air was sucked in through the neck. Microbes are like particles of dust, i.e. they are heavier than air and tend to fall slowly.

(a) Where would you expect to find microbes in the Pasteur flask?

(b) Why will the broth 'go bad' if the neck is cut off at X?

(c) List three requirements for bacterial growth.

(d) Using test tubes, an experiment was set up to imitate Pasteur's investigation. Diagram 2 shows the test tubes as they were set up. All the apparatus and the nutrient broth were sterilised in a pressure cooker.

  (i) Which tube represents the Pasteur flask?

 (ii) In which two test tubes would you expect bacteria to develop?

(iii) In which of these would you expect bacteria to develop first?

(iv) Explain your answer to (iii).

61 The diagram below shows the growth of colonies of bacteria after a fly had crawled over nutrient agar in a petri dish. Examine this diagram carefully and then answer the following questions.

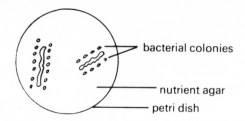

bacterial colonies

nutrient agar

petri dish

(a) From where could the fly have collected the bacteria which gave rise to these colonies?

(b) What does this suggest about ways of preventing fresh food from becoming contaminated by bacteria?

(c) What term is used for growing bacteria on agar?

(d) List four precautions necessary when growing bacteria on nutrient agar in a school laboratory.

62 Soil was thoroughly shaken up with water and the mixture filtered. The resulting solution contained soil bacteria. 10 cm³ of this filtrate was placed in each of seven test tubes, labelled Q–W. 10 cm³ of carbolic acid of different strengths was added to six of the test tubes, and 10 cm³ of water was added to the seventh. Each test tube was plugged with cotton wool and then kept at the temperatures indicated in the table. If bacteria grew in the solution, it became cloudy (turbid) and lost the odour of carbolic acid; all the clear solutions still had the odour. Examine the table carefully and then answer the questions below.

Test tube	Q	R	S	T	U	V	W
Conc. of carbolic acid	0.2%	0.1%	0.05%	0.025%	0.0125%	0.025%	water
Temperature	25 °C	25 °C	25 °C	25 °C	25 °C	10 °C	25 °C
After 7 days	clear	clear	clear	turbid	clear	clear	clear
After 14 days	clear	clear	turbid	turbid	turbid	turbid	clear

(a) In which tubes had the disinfectant not killed the bacteria after 14 days?

(b) What is the least concentration of carbolic acid that kills bacteria after 14 days?

(c) In which tube did the bacteria grow most rapidly?

(d) What do the results from tubes T and V indicate?

(e) What result would you expect if tube T was put in a refrigerator?

(f) What result would you expect if tube T had been heated in a pressure cooker at the start of the experiment?

(g) What might bacteria be using as food in test tube T?

(h) Why do no bacteria grow in W?

EXTENSION QUESTION

63 A student collected fresh leaves from three different types of tree, X, Y and Z. He cut 40 discs from each type and placed them in separate mesh bags as shown below.

The mesh bags were placed on the ground below a hedge. Samples of 10 discs were removed from each bag at monthly intervals. Each sample was crushed up in sterilised water, and equal volumes of the extract thus obtained were then put into petri dishes containing nutrient agar. These culture plates were incubated for 24 hours and the number of bacterial colonies present were recorded. The results are presented in the table below.

Leaf disc sample	Bacterial colonies			
	1st month	**2nd month**	**3rd month**	**4th month**
X	7	31	69	82
Y	5	10	32	74
Z	6	23	40	54

(a) Draw a graph of these results.

(b) Your graph should show an upward trend in the numbers of colonies for each sample. Explain this result.

(c) Why were leaf discs used instead of whole leaves?

(d) Why was sterilised water used in preparing the extract?

(e) What natural process are the bacteria carrying out on the leaves?

(f) Explain how they carry out this process.

(g) Suggest why most colonies were found from leaf extract X.

(h) Suggest two possible sources for the bacteria found in the experiment.

(i) Outline an experiment to investigate one of your suggestions.

MULTIPLE CHOICE QUESTIONS

64 Which one of the following foods does **not** directly involve microbes in its production?

A yoghurt   B cheese   C wine   D milk   E bread

65 Which one of the following foods is **not** preserved by dehydration?

A raisins
B prunes
C sultanas
D coffee
E corned beef

66 Which one of the following methods of food preservation completely sterilises the food?

A canning
B refrigeration
C freezing
D smoking
E pickling

EXTENSION QUESTION

67 Heating to a high temperature (pasteurisation) and freezing are both methods employed to preserve food. Which one of the following statements describes the essential difference between these two methods?

A Pasteurisation prevents bacteria from dividing, but freezing kills any bacteria present.
B Freezing slows down the growth rate of bacteria, while pasteurisation kills many of the bacteria present.
C Pasteurisation can only be used with milk, whereas freezing is applicable to a wide range of foodstuffs.
D Pasteurisation is less expensive than freezing.
E Freezing causes water to crystallise, which in turn causes the death of bacteria. High temperatures have no permanent effect on bacteria.

STRUCTURED QUESTIONS

68 Our food is also a good source of nutrients for microbes. When microbes live on our food, they cause it to decay and become unfit for human consumption because the microbes produce poisonous substances, called toxins. Like all organisms, microbes require the correct temperature for growth, but unlike other organisms, they are not killed by excessive cold. They are, however, killed by very high temperatures. Microbes also cannot survive if they become dehydrated or if they are put into an acid medium.

Using the above information, answer the following questions.

(a) Why are microbes in food dangerous?

(b) How does pickling in vinegar (acetic acid) ensure preservation of food?

(c) How are drying of food and jam-making related as food preservation methods?

(d) Why does food survive longer in a deep freeze than in a fridge?

(e) What method of preservation not already mentioned involves heating food to very high temperatures?

69 Some students performed an experiment to investigate the effect of temperature on yeast. They were supplied with two mixtures of dough: **R** contained plain flour, yeast and water; **S** contained plain flour, yeast, sugar and water.

They investigated four different temperatures: 3 °C, 20 °C, 35 °C and 60 °C.

Dough was poured into a measuring cylinder to a depth of 3 cm and a mark made at this level. The height of the dough above this mark was recorded every two minutes. Here is a graph of their results:

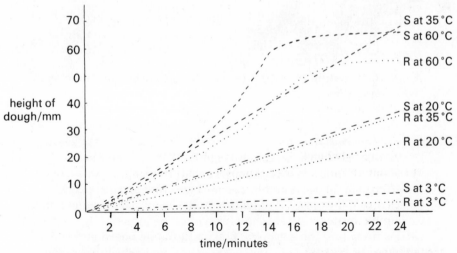

(a) Which dough always rose the most, R or S?

(b) Can you suggest why this mixture of dough gave consistently better results than the other?

(c) Which temperature is the best for rising dough?

(d) What, exactly, causes the dough to rise in this experiment?

(e) Why do you think so little happened at 3 °C?

70 In an experiment conducted in a biology class, six groups of pupils each set up three small bottles of milk and left them for a week. The three samples were: 'sterilised milk', 'pasteurised milk' and 'untreated milk', and the purpose of the experiment was to compare the effects of the different treatments on the 'keeping qualities' of milk.

When opened, all samples smelt rotten, looked clotted and, in some, the screw caps actually blew off the bottles when slackened. The main point of the investigation was therefore lost, probably due to a procedural error. The class was then asked the following questions. See if you can answer them.

(a) What organisms are responsible for making milk go bad?

(b) How do these organisms get into the milk?

(c) What results do you think might have been predicted for this experiment?

(d) What type of procedural error might have led to the observed results?

(e) The caps blew off due to a build up of gas in the bottles.
   (i) What gas do you think this was?
   (ii) What process, occurring in the organisms, was responsible for the production of this gas?
   (iii) What purpose does this process serve for the organisms?
   (iv) What else that could have been recorded or measured might have been produced by the process?

(f) The bad smell is caused by the presence of certain chemicals in the milk, and these chemicals are in some way connected with the growth of the organisms.
   (i) From where have the organisms obtained the raw materials to manufacture these chemicals?
   (ii) By what process are these bad smelling chemicals released into the milk?

71 David and Mary have invited some of their friends round for a barbecue. In case it rains, Mary decides to cook the meat early in the afternoon. Mary carries some sausages and some chicken pieces on a chopping board out to the barbecue. David cooks these for a few minutes until they are brown on the outside. He then carries them into the warm kitchen on the same board and leaves them inside. At 7.30 p.m., while the rest of the barbecue is being cooked, David puts the sausages and chicken round the edge to warm up. Their friends arrive at 8.00 p.m. to eat their meal.

David and Mary made four mistakes in their preparations which could prove dangerous. Say what these mistakes were and why each is likely to be dangerous.

72 In the manual for a new refrigerator, it says that hot food should never be put into it, but should be allowed to cool first.

    (a) Can you suggest any reason for the manufacturers giving this advice?

    (b) In a baby care manual, it explains how to make up bottles of milk from special powdered milk (called 'formula'). In these instructions, it says to use sterilised baby bottles and to use boiled water that has been slightly cooled in order to dissolve the formula.

        (i) Suggest two convenient methods for home sterilisation of the baby bottles.

        (ii) Why is boiled water used to make up the milk?

    (c) This same baby care manual recommends that the freshly-made hot bottles of baby milk be put into the fridge immediately. Can you give a good biological reason for this advice?

    (d) The fridge manual says that hot food should *not* be put into the fridge, but the baby manual says to put the hot bottles straight in. Which advice should be followed in this instance, and why?

EXTENSION QUESTION

73 Crop growth in temperate lands is seasonal, so there is obviously a need to try and preserve some of one year's yield for the winter feeding of farm animals. As in all food preservation, the object is to keep the crop in conditions which inhibit the action of microbes that would destroy the food, and to inhibit the action of enzymes within the plant material itself that would tend to decompose the food molecules present.

Two methods that attempt to do this are the making of silage and the making of hay. In silage making, the crop is cut and stored in such a way that it is partially broken down by bacteria that release lactic acid. When anaerobic conditions are maintained, the crop remains stable, further breakdown being inhibited by the low pH. In hay making, the crop is cut and allowed to dry quickly in the sun, then it is stored in dry conditions. Microbial breakdown is suppressed by the dry conditions.

Now answer the questions which follow.

    (a) In domestic situations, people use refrigerators to preserve food. Why are they not used to preserve the winter food of farm animals?

    (b) On what general principle is silage-making based, and what method of human food preservation uses the same principle?

    (c) On what general principle is hay-making based, and what human food is preserved using the same principle?

(d) Why is silage always packed down and tightly covered with a thick plastic sheet during storage?

(e) Give one disadvantage of the traditional method of hay-making in which the cut grass was spread over the field to dry?

MULTIPLE CHOICE QUESTIONS

74 Which one of the following is **not** an example of a disease caused by a microbe?

A poliomyelitis
B influenza
C measles
D whooping cough
E diabetes

75 Which one of the following conditions is caused by a microbe?

A chicken pox
B obesity
C diabetes
D rickets
E scurvy

76 In which one of the following cases is it totally impossible for a sick person to pass on their disease to anyone else?

A chicken pox
B scurvy
C AIDS
D measles
E rubella

77 In the 1860s, Joseph Lister solved the problem of preventing the infection of wounds by treating them with:

A carbonic acid
B carbolic acid
C penicillin
D interferon
E lactic acid

50

78   Alexander Fleming first showed that:

    A   sterilising under pressure destroys microbes
    B   disinfectant can inhibit bacterial growth
    C   bacteria are present in air
    D   fungi produce substances which inhibit bacterial growth
    E   bacteria can be grown on agar plates

79   A parasite is an organism that lives in or on another organism, called a host. Which of the following statements about parasites is *always* true?

    A   parasites kill their hosts
    B   parasites give their hosts disease
    C   parasites feed of their hosts
    D   parasites are larger than their hosts
    E   parasites are microscopic animals

80–81   The information in the following statement is relevant to questions 80 and 81.

Ringworm is a highly contagious fungal infection which may be spread by direct contact with people or animals that are afflicted. It takes its name from the ring-like inflamed (sore) patches on the skin.

80   What would be the best form of preventing the complaint?

    A   sterilise all individuals that have the disease
    B   avoid direct physical contact with individuals showing the disease
    C   have a regular vaccination against ringworm
    D   quarantine infected animals
    E   use a skin cream to prevent the disease

81   What would be the best way of treating this complaint?

    A   using a skin cream containing a bactericide
    B   treating affected areas with pesticide
    C   washing the sore patches in strong disinfectant
    D   applying an antifungal agent to the affected areas
    E   taking a course of vitamin C tablets

82 When you are innoculated or vaccinated against a particular disease, you are made immune to future attacks of this disease due to:

A the presence of extra white cells in the blood
B the presence of extra antigens in the blood
C the presence of extra red blood cells in the blood
D the presence of extra blood platelets in the blood
E the presence of extra antibodies in the blood

STRUCTURED QUESTIONS

83 Examine diagram I, which shows an agar plate which has been inoculated with a bacterium.

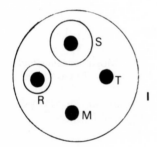
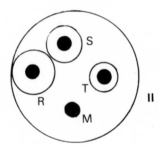

M, R, S and T are discs of paper impregnated with four different antibiotics. The clear area round each disc indicates the inhibitory effect of each antibiotic.

(a) Measure the diameter of each 'zone of inhibition' (not including the disc).
(b) Which antibiotic has no effect on this bacterium?
(c) Which antibiotic has the greatest effect on this bacterium?

Diagram II shows the effect of the same antibiotic on a different bacterium.

(d) Measure the diameter of each 'zone of inhibition' (not including the disc).
(e) If a person was suffering from an infection of both bacteria, which would be the best antibiotic to give them?
(f) Explain your answer to (e).

84 The following diagram illustrates a simplified life cycle of the parasite which causes malaria.

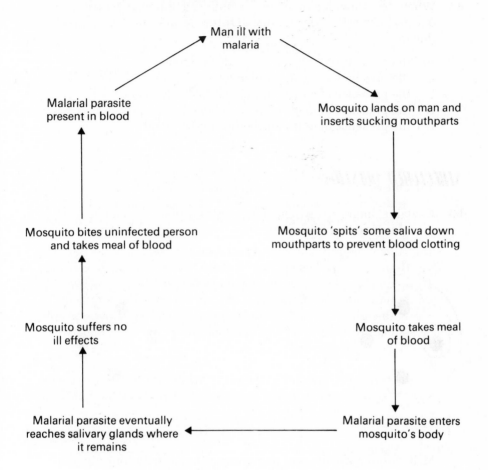

(a) How many hosts does the malarial parasite have?
(b) To which one does it cause damage?
(c) Why is the mosquito called the *vector* of the disease?
(d) Can you become infected with malaria by direct contact with someone suffering from it?
(e) Explain carefully how the parasite gets into the mosquito.
(f) What part of the insect does the parasite enter first?
(g) Where does it finally live in the mosquito?
(h) Explain carefully how the parasite is transferred from the mosquito into a person.

85 Malaria is a disease transmitted by a mosquito (Anopheles). This mosquito lives in many countries, including Britain. The mosquito larvae and pupae live in water. The following are diagrams of a larva and a pupa.

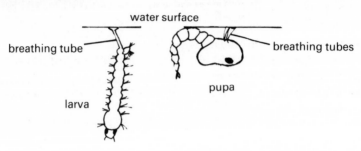

(a) One of the ways of eradicating malaria is to destroy the larvae and pupae. Look carefully at the diagrams and explain why spraying the surface of the water with oil will kill larvae and pupae.

(b) Why would this be a better method of controlling the parasite than spraying houses, etc., with an insecticide, such as DDT?

(c) Britain has been free of local malaria since 1911. However, holiday-makers returning to Britain are sometimes infected with malaria. What would be the result of one of these people being bitten by an Anopheles mosquito after he or she had returned to Britain?

Look at the following table of figures, which shows the deaths (in millions) due to malaria in the years 1972, 1974, 1976 and 1978.

World regions	Deaths/millions			
	1972	1974	1976	1978
Africa	3.995	5.120	5.212	5.330
Americas	0.285	0.269	0.379	0.465
S.E. Asia	1.816	4.162	7.296	4.264
Europe	0.013	0.007	0.041	0.093
Eastern Mediterranean	0.830	0.480	0.347	0.126

(d) In which part of the world did malaria show a continuous decrease between 1972 and 1978?

(e) In which parts of the world, between 1972 and 1978, did malaria show first a decrease and then an increase again?

(f) Offer one explanation for the rise in death figures for Africa.

86 German measles (*Rubella*) is not a serious disease, except for unborn babies.

(a) How might an unborn baby contract this disease?

(b) What natural method of protection might a pregnant woman have against *Rubella*?

(c) What artificial method of protection could be used to protect against the disease?

(d) When would be a suitable time for this method to be used?

(e) Give one advantage of men being protected against *Rubella*.

87 The map below shows the Soho district of London as it was in 1854, with water pumps (the only source of water) marked as black circles. The numbers show the numbers of people who died from cholera over a period of 10 days in September, as recorded by Dr John Snow

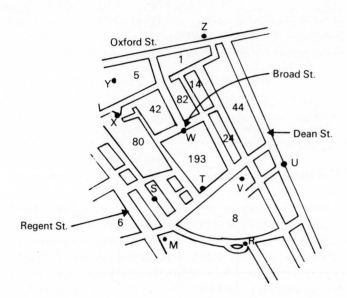

(a) Give the letter of the water pump which you think was the most likely source of the outbreak.

(b) What led you to this conclusion?

(c) From this information how do you think cholera is spread?

(d) How could the outbreak have been controlled?

(e) Suggest why the epidemic started in the first place.

(f) Suggest why the epidemic killed so many people.

88 Smallpox is a disease which disfigures, blinds and kills. In 1796 Edward Jenner first vaccinated people against smallpox using pus (fluid) from the sore caused by a milder disease—cowpox. In 1800 the first smallpox vaccination was carried out in America. In 1959 the World Health Organisation (WHO) decided to try and wipe out smallpox altogether.

The following table shows the last naturally-occurring cases of smallpox in the world.

Date	World region
1970	West Africa
1971	Brazil and Central Africa
1973	Afghanistan
1974	Pakistan
1975	Nepal, India, Bangladesh
1976	Ethiopia
1977	Kenya, Somalia

(a) How many years passed from Jenner's vaccination until smallpox was finally wiped out?

(b) After the WHO decision, in which world region did smallpox first disappear?

(c) Which country recorded its last case of smallpox in 1973?

(d) How does vaccination give protection against a disease such as smallpox?

(e) Why is it still necessary to retain supplies of the smallpox vaccine?

89 Tuberculosis (TB) is a disease caused by a bacterium which can be found in cow's milk, or the bacterium may be inhaled in water droplets from the air. It can affect all the organs in the body, although it generally attacks the lungs most severely. Sometimes, it has little apparent effect on the body, although in its most serious form it is fatal. It may damage the lungs and this may not be obvious until an X-ray examination is made.
TB can be controlled in individual patients by the use of antibiotics, and prevented by means of the BCG vaccination. Between 1932 and 1970, the number of TB cases in Britain fell from 45 000 to just under 12 000.

(a) List four ways in which the fall in the number of TB cases may have been brought about.

(b) Suppose a number of primary school children in one class only became infected with TB. How could you find out if the infection came from milk or was inhaled?

(c) What name is given to the process used in dairies by which TB bacteria are destroyed in milk?

(d) Outline one method of doing this.

EXTENSION QUESTION

90 Rabies is a deadly disease that can be transmitted by the bite of a rabid animal. Imported animals are vaccinated against the disease while being kept in quarantine for six months. Rabies is not found in Australia, New Zealand, Japan, Malta, Cyprus and the British Isles, but is found in most other countries of the world.

(a) Why do you think imported animals are vaccinated against rabies?

(b) Why do you think they are quarantined?

(c) Why do you think the quarantine period is six months?

(d) Why do countries on the European mainland not have quarantine regulations?

(e) How do you account for the named countries being free of this disease?

Theme 3
Maintenance and Organisation

MULTIPLE CHOICE QUESTIONS

1 Which of the following is a characteristic of plant cells only?

   A   cell membrane
   B   cell wall
   C   cytoplasm
   D   nucleus
   E   protoplasm

2 Which one of the following sets of characteristics is common to both a palisade cell of a leaf and a human cheek cell?

   A   cell wall, nucleus, chloroplasts
   B   chloroplasts, cell membrane, nucleus
   C   cell wall, cell membrane, nucleus
   D   cell membrane, cytoplasm, nucleus
   E   cell wall, cell membrane, chloroplasts

3 The following diagram shows a plant and an animal cell.

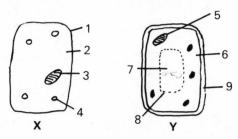

   Which features of Y indicate that it is a plant cell?

   A   7, 8, 9   B   5, 6, 8   C   6, 7, 8   D   5, 6, 7   E   5, 7, 9

4 In multicellular organisms, cells become specialised to perform different functions. Which combination of cells perform, between them, all the functions in the following list?

   transport of oxygen, support, transport of water, protection

   A   phloem, xylem, epidermis
   B   white blood cells, xylem, skin
   C   red blood cells, xylem, epidermis
   D   red blood cells, phloem, epidermis
   E   bone, red blood cells, skin

EXTENSION QUESTION

5   Cells become specialised for different functions in the human body. White blood cells, nerve cells and sperm cells are examples of such specialised cells.

Which one of the following lists of functions is carried out by these three types of cells?

A   protection, transport of O_2, reproduction
B   transport of O_2, transmission of impulses, support
C   protection, transmission of impulses, reproduction
D   transport of O_2, transport of CO_2, protection
E   transport of CO_2, transmission of impulses, reproduction

STRUCTURED QUESTIONS

6   Examine diagram 1, which shows a microscope.

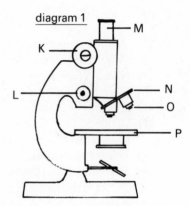

diagram 1

(a) Name the parts labelled K–P.
(b) If the magnification of M is × 10 and the magnification of O is × 40, by how much will an object be magnified if it is viewed through these two?

(c) Diagram 2 shows the field of view observed by a pupil as she looks through a microscope at some cells. Using the letters from the drawings, indicate which is:
   (i) low power;
  (ii) medium power;
  (iii) high power.

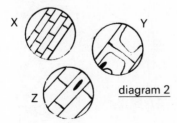

diagram 2

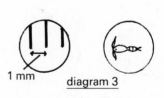

1 mm

diagram 3

(d) Diagram 3 shows the millimetre scale of a ruler and a microscopic pond animal. Estimate the actual size of the animal. Show your working.

c

7 The internal structure of cells can be seen using a microscope. Below are two diagrams of cells. X is seen using a light microscope and Y is seen using the much more powerful electron microscope.

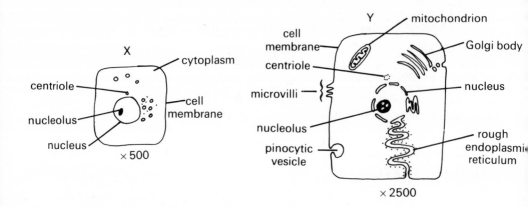

(a) What is the magnification of X?
(b) What is the magnification of Y?
(c) Name three structures which can be seen in both X and Y.
(d) Give two differences between the nuclei of X and Y.
(e) Name two structures which can only be seen in Y.
(f) What structure seen in Y provides a passageway from outside the cell to the nucleus?
(g) What two adaptations of the cell membrane can be seen in Y?
(h) Give one way in which these could be of benefit to the cell.
(i) What structure seen in Y allows the cell to secrete to the outside?

8 Examine the following diagrams which show three cells: X, Y and Z.

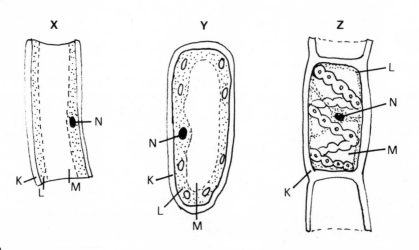

(a) The structures labelled K–M are comparable for all three cell types shown. Identify each structure.

(b) Which two cells are photosynthetic?

(c) Why do you think the other cell is not photosynthetic?

(d) Which cell has come from the mesophyll of a leaf?

(e) Give one difference between the two photosynthetic cells.

9 The following are characteristics of animal cells.

no cell wall	cytoplasm
cell membrane	nucleus
irregular shape	no large vacuole

The diagrams below all show plant and animal cells.

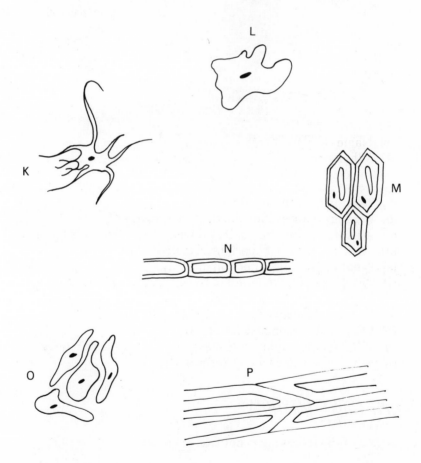

(a) Write down the letters of those which are plant cells.

(b) Write down the letters of those which are animal cells.

(c) Identify the cells labelled K, L and N.

10 The following diagrams show a variety of plant cells with their names.

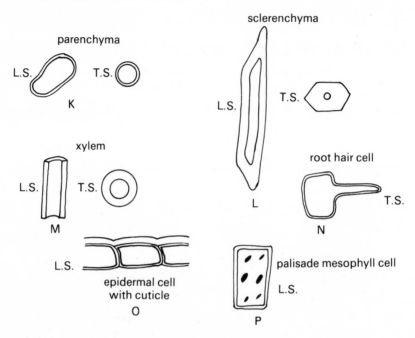

(a) What is the function of O?
(b) What structures indicate the function of P?
(c) What is the function of P and where are these cells found?
(d) Which is the least specialised cell?
(e) What is the major function of L?
(f) The fibres of L are found in the stems and trunks of plants. Explain why they are suited to this.
(g) What is the major function of M?
(h) What is its secondary function?
(i) What features allow it to carry out both these functions?
(j) Why does N have a very large surface area?

MULTIPLE CHOICE QUESTIONS

11 Which of the following is **not** true of enzymes?

    A   they only act on specific substrates
    B   they are affected by pH
    C   they are needed in large quantities
    D   they are affected by temperature
    E   they occur in living organisms

12 Which of the following will **not** affect the action of the enzyme amylase?

A pH
B temperature
C concentration of the substrate
D concentration of the enzyme
E atmospheric pressure

13 The enzyme amylase, in saliva, breaks down:

A cellulose B fat C protein D starch E sugar

14 Which one of the following correctly shows an enzyme and its substrate?

	Substrate	Enzyme
A	lipase	glycerol
B	protein	protease
C	carbohydrase	carbohydrate
D	protease	carbohydrase
E	amino acid	lipase

15 Which one of the following combinations of temperature and pH will give the best conditions for a protein-digesting enzyme found in the stomach?

A 37 °C—pH 2.0
B 25 °C—pH 3.0
C 37 °C—pH 7.0
D 50 °C—pH 2.0
E 37 °C—pH 9.0

16 A solution of hydrogen peroxide, left by itself, will slowly break down into water and oxygen. If an enzyme is added, however, this breakdown occurs much more quickly. In this reaction, hydrogen peroxide is the:

A protein
B product
C catalyst
D enzyme
E substrate

17 There is a substance in bananas called polyphenol oxidase, which, when oxygen is present, turns food molecules in the banana cells into dark-coloured products which make the banana go brown or black. Which of the following would be a logical way of establishing whether polyphenol oxidase is an enzyme or not?

A   see if unpeeled bananas go black
B   boil the banana and see if it goes black
C   deprive the banana of oxygen and see if it goes black
D   see if the banana goes black in the absence of carbon dioxide
E   see if the banana goes black in an atmosphere of pure nitrogen

STRUCTURED QUESTIONS

18 Enzymes are organic catalysts that are found widely in the living world, controlling the biochemical reactions that occur in living things. Enzymes act on molecules called *substrates* to make molecules called *products*.

(a) Name one digestive enzyme and say what its substrate and product molecules are.
(b) Name one biological process besides digestion which involves enzymes.
(c) List the factors that might affect the rate of any given enzyme-controlled reaction.
(d) What effect would boiling have on the activity of an enzyme? Explain.

19 The rate of an enzyme-controlled reaction was measured at different temperatures. All other factors were kept constant. The results are presented in the following table.

Temperature/°C	5	15	25	35	45	55	65
Rate of reaction /arbitrary units	0	4	27	74	72	6	0

(a) Plot a fully-labelled graph of these data, joining the points up with an appropriate smooth curve.
(b) Why do you think the reaction rate is zero at 5 °C?
(c) Why do you think the reaction rate is zero at 65 °C?
(d) What do you think is:
   (i) the optimum temperature?
   (ii) the maximum rate for this reaction?

(e) What do you think would be the rate of reaction at:
   (i) 30 °C?
   (ii) 50 °C?

20 A pupil is investigating the effect of salivary amylase on starch. First of all, he places a drop of iodine into each of the twelve depressions in a spotting tile. He then rinses his mouth with distilled water and chews for two minutes on a clean rubber band. Next, he mixes 2 cm³ of saliva, 2 cm³ of starch suspension and 1 cm³ of air in a plastic syringe.
At 30 second intervals, he expels a few drops of this mixture into a depression on the spotting tile so that it mixes with the iodine. At first, the iodine drops turn dark blue almost immediately, but the 5th and 6th drops do so more slowly and the 10th, 11th and 12th drops fail to change colour at all when the saliva and starch mixture is added.

(a) What colour is iodine solution?
(b) Why did the pupil wash out his mouth with distilled water?
(c) What was the purpose of chewing on the rubber band?
(d) Why was 1 cm³ air drawn into the syringe along with the saliva and starch?
(e) Why did the first few drops of iodine turn blue quickly?
(f) Why did the 5th and 6th drops change colour more slowly?
(g) Why did the 10th, 11th and 12th drops fail to change colour at all?
(h) Describe how you would find out if the saliva had converted the starch into a simple sugar.

21 Two amylase enzymes were allowed to act on starch. The amount of sugar produced (expressed as a percentage of the original starch quantity) after thirty minutes at different temperatures is shown in the table below.

	Percentage of starch turned to sugar after 30 minutes									
Enzyme M	4	8	13	24	46	62	61	58	51	36	6
Enzyme N	7	19	33	56	57	54	31	20	11	5	0
Temp./°C	10	15	20	25	30	35	40	45	50	55	60

(a) Plot these results as two line graphs on the same set of axes (temperature on x-axis).
(b) What is the optimum temperature for enzyme M?

(c) What is the effect on this enzyme of increasing the temperature above the optimum?

(d) What is the optimum temperature for enzyme N?

(e) What is the effect on this enzyme of increasing the temperature above the optimum?

(f) Which enzyme is completely deactivated at 60 °C?

(g) Give a reason for your answer to **(f)**.

(h) Give one other difference between the effect of temperature on the two enzymes.

(i) One of the enzymes came from a mammal. Say which one, and give a reason for your choice.

22 The following experiment was set up to test the effect of pH on the activity of pepsin. Pepsin is a protein-digesting enzyme found in the stomach. The pH in the stomach is around 2.0.

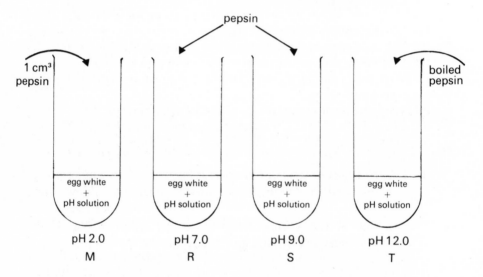

(a) From the information, what type of food substance is egg white?

(b) 1 cm³ pepsin was added to test-tube M. How much would be added to test-tubes R and S?

(c) How much boiled pepsin would be added to T?

(d) What do you know about the amount of the pH solutions added to tubes M–T?

(e) In which tube would you expect the egg white to be digested fastest?

(f) Explain your answer to **(e)**.

(g) Why was test-tube T set up?

(h) The test-tubes were set in a water bath during the experiment.
  (i) What temperature should the bath be kept at?
  (ii) Why?

23 Some washing powders are described as having a 'biological' action because they contain enzymes. These powders are particularly useful for removing stains such as blood, egg, chocolate and gravy. However, the manufacturers suggest that such washing powders are most effective in warm water, i.e. water at body temperature, rather than hot water. The powders are much less effective if boiling water is used.

(a) List four properties of enzymes.

(b) Why do you think enzymes would be most effective against stains like those listed above?

(c) Approximately what temperature in, °C, is 'warm' water?

(d) Suggest a reason why biological powders are less effective at higher temperatures.

(e) What other advantage of a social or economic nature do biological washing powders have over non-biological washing powders?

MULTIPLE CHOICE QUESTIONS

24 Which one of the following is the best definition of osmosis?

A   the movement of water from cell to cell

B   the movement of solvent molecules from a region of low solute concentration to a region of high solute concentration

C   the movement of solute molecules from a region of low solute concentration to a region of high solvent concentration

D   the movement of solvent molecules from a region of high solute concentration to a region of low solute concentration through a selectively permeable membrane

E   the movement of solvent molecules from a region of low solute concentration to a region of high solute concentration through a selectively permeable membrane

25 When red blood cells are added to water, the cells burst. The reason for this is:

A   red blood cells cannot survive outside the human body

B   red blood cells react with an antibody present in the water

C   red blood cells lose water to the surrounding water by osmosis

D   red blood cells gain water from the surrounding water by osmosis

E   red blood cells are crushed by atmospheric pressure

26 The kidneys are important in regulating body fluids. They do this by excreting:

- A   excess glucose, excess water, salts
- B   urea, excess water, excess salts
- C   unwanted proteins, excess water, excess salts
- D   excess amino acids, excess water, unwanted solutes
- E   urea, excess amino acids, excess ammonia

27 The kidney is said to be an osmoregulatory organ because:

- A   it keeps the osmotic potential of the blood more or less constant
- B   it carries out osmosis
- C   it regulates the rate of osmosis
- D   it keeps the osmotic potential of urine more or less constant
- E   it keeps the osmotic potential of blood and urine more or less constant

28 It has been estimated that the entire fluid environment of the body (approximately 10 litres) passes through a pair of human kidneys 15 times in 24 hours. During the same period of time, the kidneys may produce approximately 1 litre of urine. This indicates that:

- A   the bladder receives the urine and returns most of it to the body
- B   the kidneys leak so that urine passes into the blood
- C   all of the filtrate in the kidneys is reabsorbed
- D   most fluid passing through the kidneys is reabsorbed
- E   it takes 150 litres of body fluid to make 1 litre of urine

EXTENSION QUESTION

29 Which one of the following **cannot** be explained by osmosis?

- A   the movement of water from the soil to root hairs
- B   the collapsing of onion epidermal cells in strong sugar solution
- C   the movement of glucose from the blood stream into respiring cells
- D   the swelling up of a visking tube 'sausage' of sugar solution in water
- E   the movement of water through cells of the root cortex

30 The diagram below shows a simplified section through part of a root.

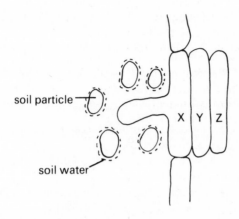

(a) Name two substances which might be dissolved in the cell sap of X.

(b) If the soil water surrounding X contains very few dissolved substances, i.e. is less concentrated than the cell sap, explain the direction in which water molecules will move.

(c) How will the movement in **(b)** affect the concentration of cell X relative to cell Y?

(d) What are the consequences of the change outlined in **(c)**?

(e) If the same root system was placed into water with a high salt content, explain how this would affect the movement of water molecules between the soil and cell X.

(f) On the basis of your answer to **(e)**, say why it is that few plants can grow in soil which is very close to the sea, even if the soil is high in plant nutrients.

31 A teacher attempted to demonstrate osmosis using the largest cell she could find. Two chicken eggs were first placed in dilute hydrochloric acid (HCl) overnight to dissolve their shells. (HCl does not damage the membrane of the egg.)

The volumes of the two 'soft' eggs were now measured using an overflow can borrowed from the physics department. The first egg was then placed into a large beaker of distilled water, while the second was placed into a large beaker of very salty water.

Two days later the eggs were retrieved and their volumes measured again. Here are the results:

Initial volume of first egg	$62\,cm^3$
Initial volume of second egg	$57\,cm^3$
Final volume of first egg	$69\,cm^3$
Final volume of second egg	$51\,cm^3$

(a) How has the volume of the first egg changed after two days?
(b) Explain your answer to (a).
(c) How has the volume of the second egg changed after two days?
(d) Explain your answer to (c).
(e) Suggest what might happen to the second egg if, after the two day period, it was placed into distilled water.
(f) Why was it necessary to remove the shell at the beginning of the experiment?

32 Visking tubing is an artificial material which is transparent and flexible when wet. It allows water molecules to pass through easily, but sugar molecules much less easily.

In an experiment to investigate the effect of osmosis, a pupil constructed a 'sausage' from visking tubing and filled it with strong sugar solution. The 'sausage' was then tightly tied and its outer surface rinsed with distilled water, before being carefully dried and weighed. The 'sausage' was placed into a beaker of distilled water for one hour and was then retrieved, dried and weighed again.

The following were the results obtained:

Mass before placing in distilled water	$13.1\,g$
Mass after 1 hour in distilled water	$15.3\,g$

(a) Suggest why visking tubing allows water molecules to pass through more easily than sugar molecules.
(b) What parts of plant and animal cells have similar properties to visking tubing?
(c) Why was it necessary to rinse the 'sausage' with distilled water?
(d) Why was it essential to dry it before each weighing?
(e) Calculate the exact change in mass.

(f) Calculate the percentage change in mass.

(g) Can you explain why the mass changed in the way that it did?

(h) What other change do you think you might observe, apart from the change in mass?

(i) What word is used to describe the state of a plant cell which is in a similar state to the visking tube at the end of the experiment?

33 Read the following lines carefully:

> *If your lettuce is not in good nick*
> *All floppy and decidedly sick*
> *Don't nurse it*
> *Or curse it*
> *But in water immerse it*
> *_ _ _ _ _ _ will do the trick!*

(a) What is the missing word in the last line? (*Hint*: it is the name of an important biological process.)

(b) What might have caused the lettuce to become all 'floppy' in the first place?

(c) What biological term can be used for 'floppy' when applied to leaves?

(d) When taken out of the water, the lettuce leaves might be described as 'crisp'. What word could be used to describe the condition of the *cells* in the leaves?

(e) What would happen to lettuce leaves that were immersed in a strong sugar solution?

(f) Explain your answer to **(e)**.

34 The young seedlings of most plants have extremely delicate, thin stems which hold aloft the developing leaves. These stems contain no woody strengthening material. Young seedlings should always be handled by the seed leaves and not by the stem when they are being transplanted. Seedlings should only be transplanted after they have been well-watered, and preferably in the evening rather than in the morning.

(a) If seedlings contain no woody material, what enables them to remain upright?

(b) Why should seedlings only be handled by the leaves and not by the stem?

(c) Why should seedlings be well-watered prior to being transplanted?

(d) Why is it preferable to transplant seedlings in the evening rather than in the morning?

35 The diagram below shows a portion of the human kidney.

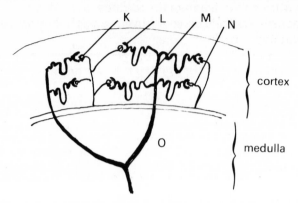

The following table gives some information about substances found in blood capillaries and kidney tubules.

	Blood	**Liquid in tubule**
Glucose	✓	✓
Amino acids	✓	✓
Blood cells	✓	
Plasma proteins	✓	

(a) Which letter on the above diagram indicates a capillary?

(b) Which letters on the above diagram indicate parts of a kidney tubule?

(c) Which substances are present in the capillary and absent from the tubule?

(d) What process accounts for this?

(e) Between which two letters on the diagram does this occur?

(f) What is the function of the structure labelled O?

36 The following is a diagram of a kidney nephron (tubule).

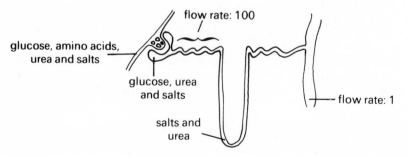

(a) What substances listed as present in the blood are absent from the filtrate which enters the tubule?

(b) What substance is later removed completely from the tubule?

(c) What happens to this substance?

(d) If flow rate is a measure of the amount of water present, which is more concentrated: the liquid in the tubule or the liquid in the collecting duct?

(e) If a person loses a lot of blood in an accident, the kidneys may stop functioning. As soon as blood is given to the patient, the kidneys begin functioning again. What does this tell you about what 'drives' the liquid from the capillaries into the Bowman's capsule?

37 A small unicellular organism lives close to the mouth of a river (an estuary) and, consequently, has problems related to the changes in the salt content of its surroundings. The following graph shows changes in the volume of the organism during a twenty four hour period.

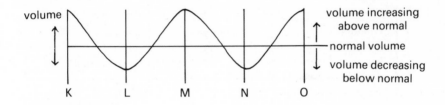

(a) What happens to the salt content of the water in the estuary when:

    (i) the tide is fully out?

    (ii) the tide is fully in?

(b) Between which points on the graph is the organism:

    (i) losing water?

    (ii) gaining water?

(c) By what process does the animal absorb and lose water?

(d) Some unicellular animals have a special structure for removing excess water from their bodies. What is it called?

(e) What is happening to the tide when:

    (i) the animal is losing water?

    (ii) the animal is gaining water?

38 The following diagram illustrates kidney tubules from five groups of vertebrates. The tubules are drawn vertically, with the loops of Henlé straightened out.

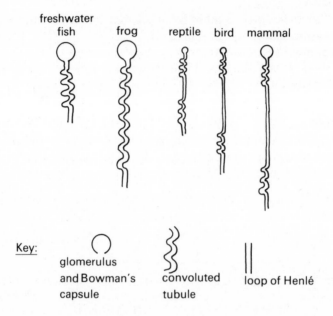

The quantity of urine produced and its concentration depend on two things:

    1 the rate of filtration of the blood into the Bowman's capsule;
    2 the amount of water reabsorbed by the kidney.

The rate of filtration is partly governed by the size of the Bowman's capsule. The amount of water reabsorbed depends on the length of the loop of Henlé.

Answer the following questions.

(a) In which animals is the loop of Henlé present?
(b) Which animals have the longest loops of Henlé?
(c) Which animals have the smallest Bowman's capsules?
(d) In which animals will the rate of filtration be highest?
(e) Give a reason for your answer to **(d)**.
(f) What structure enables birds and mammals to produce concentrated urine?
(g) Freshwater fish live in a dilute environment and tend to take in water through their skin by osmosis. Why do they not have a loop of Henlé?

39 Which one of the following elements is particularly required for the formation of chlorophyll?

A   iron
B   calcium
C   manganese
D   nitrogen
E   magnesium

40 Which one of the following word equations best represents photosynthesis?

A   carbon + water + light absorbed→carbohydrate + oxygen
    dioxide   by chlorophyll

B   carbohydrate + oxygen→energy + carbon + water
                                        dioxide

C   carbon + water + light reflected →carbohydrate + oxygen
    dioxide   by chlorophyll

D   carbon + hydrogen + water + radiant→carbohydrate
                                energy

E   carbon + oxygen + light absorbed→carbohydrate + water
    dioxide   by chlorophyll

41 When a freshly picked geranium leaf is dropped into a beaker of boiling water, large numbers of small bubbles are observed rising from the lower surface of the leaf. Which one of the following best explains this observation?

A   there are more stomata on the lower epidermis than on the upper epidermis
B   the pores on the upper surface close automatically in response to high temperature
C   most of the chloroplasts are found nearer the upper epidermis
D   there are more stomata on the upper epidermis than on the lower epidermis
E   stomata are equally distributed on the upper and lower surface of the geranium leaves

42 A green leaf is covered by a lightproof stencil and placed in a CO_2 free atmosphere beside a lamp. If this leaf is later tested for starch with iodine solution, which of the following results would you expect?

	Shaded area of leaf	Exposed area of leaf
A	green	green
B	blue-black	brown
C	blue-black	blue-black
D	brown	brown
E	brown	blue-black

43 Dry rot and wet rot are fungal infestations of building timbers such as window frames and floor joists. The reason why these organisms can survive in such places is because:

A they produce their own food by photosynthesis
B they feed saprophytically on their surroundings
C they feed heterotrophically on surrounding insects
D they feed parasitically on surrounding organisms
E they feed automatically

44 Sometimes if plants lose too much water during the day, their stomata will close to restrict further water loss. However, this daytime stomatal closure may influence the rate of photosynthesis by restricting carbon dioxide diffusion into the leaf.
Which one of the following do you think is the most likely outcome of this stomatal closure?

A no influence on the rate of photosynthesis
B increase the rate of photosynthesis
C decrease the rate of photosynthesis
D at first increase and then decrease the rate of photosynthesis
E at first decrease and then increase the rate of photosynthesis

45–47 The diagram which follows refers to questions 45–47. Examine the diagram and then answer the questions.

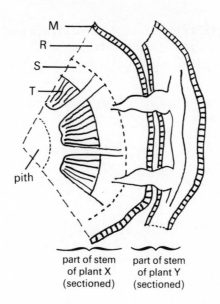

part of stem
of plant X
(sectioned)

part of stem
of plant Y
(sectioned)

45 Which of the following is the correct combination of structures
indicated by the letters?

	M	R	S	T
A	epidermis	phloem	xylem	cortex
B	epidermis	cortex	phloem	xylem
C	phloem	xylem	cortex	epidermis
D	phloem	cortex	xylem	epidermis
E	epidermis	cortex	xylem	phloem

46 Which of the pairs of relationships given below is shown by plants
X and Y?

	X	Y
A	saprophyte	parasite
B	host	epiphyte
C	parasite	host
D	host	parasite
E	saprophyte	epiphyte

EXTENSION QUESTION

47 Match the lettered tissues for plant X with the correct functions.

	M	R	S	T
A	protection	food transport	water transport	packing
B	packing	food transport	water transport	protection
C	protection	packing	food transport	water transport
D	packing	water transport	food transport	protection
E	protection	packing	water transport	food transport

STRUCTURED QUESTIONS

48 Examine the following diagram of a flowering plant.

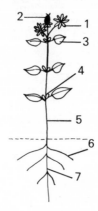

(a) Name the numbered parts.
(b) Match the numbered parts to the correct description of their functions from the following list.
    (i) Absorbs nutrients from the soil.
   (ii) May give rise to a flower or branch.
  (iii) May store food.
  (iv) Produces seeds.
   (v) Holds seeds before dispersal.
  (vi) Traps radiant energy.
 (vii) Displays flowers and leaves above ground.

49 The diagram below shows a cross-section through a plant stem.

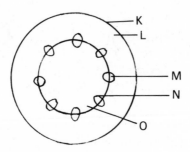

(a) Name the structures labelled K–O.
(b) What is the function of tissue M?
(c) What is the main function of tissue N?
(d) What name is given to groups of tissues M and N?
(e) What kind of cells occupy region O?
(f) Does this cross-section represent a monocotyledon or a dicotyledon? Give your reason.

50   Examine the following diagram.

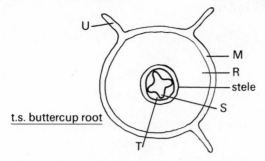

t.s. buttercup root

(a) Identify the structures indicated on the diagram.
(b) Match these structures with the functions listed below:
   (i) absorption of water;
  (ii) storage of food;
 (iii) transport of food;
 (iv) transport of water;
  (v) protection
(c) What general term is applied to a collection of cells that make up *any* of the structures labelled?
(d) What general term is applied to the *collection* of *cells* which includes *all* of the structures labelled?
(e) What general term is applied to a collection of structures, such as a tap root and lateral roots, found on the same plant?

51   Use the letters on the following diagram to answer the questions below (some letters may be needed more than once).

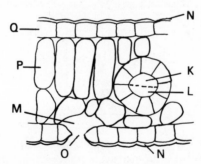

(a) Where does the carbon dioxide enter the leaf?
(b) Where is the leaf waterproofed?
(c) Where is carbon dioxide used?
(d) Where does photosynthesis occur?
(e) Where does most of the water leave the leaf?
(f) Where is oxygen produced?
(g) Where are there the largest number of chloroplasts?
(h) Where is the waterproof layer produced?
(i) Where may water vapour and gases be retained in the leaf?

52 It is sometimes necessary to test leaves of plants for the presence of starch.

   (a) After the leaf is cut from the plant, it is usually killed before proceeding with the test.
   (i) How is the leaf killed?
   (ii) Why is the leaf killed?

   (b) The next step generally involves decolourising the leaf.
   (i) How is the leaf decolourised?
   (ii) Why is the leaf decolourised?

   (c) What is the significance of testing a variegated leaf for the presence of starch?

   (d) What would be the effect of coating a leaf with Vaseline two days before it is detached and tested for starch? How do you explain this effect?

53 The rate of photosynthesis of an aquatic plant such as Canadian pondweed (*Elodea*) can be conveniently measured by counting the number of bubbles evolved by a sprig of the plant in a given time interval.
The diagram below shows such an arrangement. An immersion heater with a variable output allows the temperature of the water to be altered.

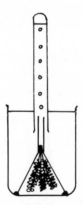

The table below shows the number of bubbles counted in 2 minute intervals at several temperatures. *Note:* An interval of five minutes elapsed at each new temperature before the bubbles were counted.

Temperature/°C	5	10	15	20	25	30	35
Number of bubbles/2 mins	13	25	37	48	60	57	52

   (a) Name the gas which formed the bubbles being counted.
   (b) How could you confirm your answer to **(a)**?

(c) Construct a graph of temperature (horizontal axis) against number of bubbles (vertical axis).

(d) Why was a 5 minute interval allowed to elapse at each new temperature before the bubbles were counted?

(e) What is the optimum temperature for the photosynthesis of *Elodea*?

(f) If room temperature is 18 °C, use your graph to estimate the number of bubbles produced in a two minute period at room temperature.

(g) Suggest two further factors which could alter the rate of photosynthesis of *Elodea*.

54 The graph below shows the rate of photosynthesis in green and variegated leaves at different light intensities.

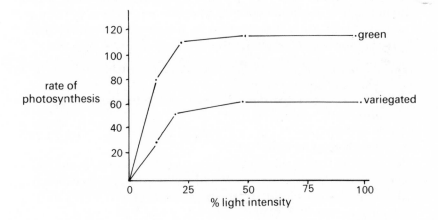

(a) Explain why green leaves have a higher rate of photosynthesis than variegated leaves.

(b) Account for the shape of the curve for green leaves.

(c) Why do you think green privet bushes, commonly used as a hedging plant, need to be clipped more often than variegated privet bushes?

(d) The variegated privet bush is usually found to have a few branches on which all the leaves are completely yellow. Explain how such leaves are nourished.

(e) Why do you think variegated forms of perennial plants usually break their winter rest period earlier in the spring than the green forms?

55   In an experiment to determine whether or not chlorophyll is
essential for photosynthesis, a student decides to use leaves of the
common houseplant *Chlorophytum*, commonly known as the
spider plant. The leaves are long and narrow and consist of
alternate green and white stripes, as illustrated in the diagram
below.

A complete plant was first kept in the dark for 24 hours. It was
then brightly illuminated under a Gro-lamp for 3 hours. At the end
of this period, the leaf was tested for the presence of starch using
the standard starch-iodine test.

(a) What name is used to describe plants whose leaves have both
white and green regions?

(b) Why was the experimental plant kept in the dark for 24 hours
prior to the experiment?

(c) Why was it necessary to illuminate the plant for 3 hours, rather
than just a few minutes?

(d) What is the significance of the presence of starch in the leaf?

(e) Describe briefly how you would test for the presence of starch.

(f) Redraw the leaf illustrated and indicate on it the distribution
of colours which would be observed when the test was
completed.

56   An experiment to investigate the effect of light on the uptake of
carbon dioxide by green plants was set up by two students, 'X'
and 'Y'.

Student X's method: Take three test-tubes.
Place bicarbonate indicator solution in
each.
Put one leaf in each tube.
Put two tubes on the window sill.
Put the third tube in a cupboard.
Leave for twenty-four hours.

Student Y's method: Take three test-tubes.
Label them A, B and C.
Cut six leaf discs from the same leaf
of a plant.
Place 5 cm³ bicarbonate indicator solution
in each test-tube.
Put three leaf discs in A and B.
Cover B with tinfoil.
Place all three tubes in light.
Leave for twenty-four hours.

(a) Which experiment is more scientifically precise?
(b) Pick out three steps from this experiment and explain why you think they are more accurate.
(c) Which student set up a control?
(d) What was the control?
(e) What results would you expect from the three test-tubes in Students Y's experiment?
(f) Explain your three answers to **(e)**.

EXTENSION QUESTION

57 Examine the following diagram carefully. It illustrates the apparatus used in an experiment investigating photosynthesis in a green leaf.

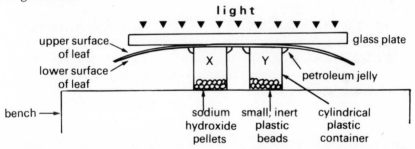

As you can see, a leaf has two small containers pressed against its lower surface and a glass plate pressing down on top. It is left in the light for 6 hours then the entire leaf is taken and tested for the presence of starch.

(a) What is the function of the sodium hydroxide pellets in container X?
(b) What is the function of the plastic beads in container Y?
(c) What is the function of the petroleum jelly which surrounds the join between each container and the leaf?
(d) Why do you think the containers are attached to the lower surface rather than the upper surface?

(e) What chemical reagent would be used to test for starch?

(f) How should the leaf be treated before the test is carried out to ensure that the results are clearly visible?

(g) Draw a diagram to show clearly which parts of the leaf would contain starch and which would not after testing.

(h) What conclusion would you draw from these results?

(i) To ensure the validity of this conclusion, how should the leaf be treated prior to the experiment and why?

MULTIPLE CHOICE QUESTIONS

58 In which one of the following parts of the digestive system is gastric juice produced?

A duodenum
B stomach
C mouth
D ileum
E oesophagus

59 When food enters the digestive system, it passes through the following parts before it is completely digested.

duodenum	mouth	stomach	ileum	oesophagus
1	2	3	4	5

Which of the following indicates the correct order?

A 1, 2, 3, 4, 5
B 2, 5, 3, 4, 1
C 2, 5, 3, 1, 4
D 3, 1, 2, 5, 4
E 2, 3, 5, 1, 4

60 A food mixture is found to give a positive result with both the Biuret test and the iodine test, but a negative result when tested with Benedict's solution. The mixture is most likely to be:

A vegetable oil and milk
B chocolate and apple
C water and sweet black tea
D cheese and flour
E ham and eggs

61 The dental formula of an adult human is $\dfrac{2123}{2123}$. Given this information, which one of the following statements **cannot** be logically made?

A humans have a single canine tooth in the upper jaw
B humans have twelve molars in total
C humans have the same number of teeth in the upper jaw as in the lower jaw
D humans have thirty two teeth in total
E humans have four incisors in the lower jaw

62 Which one of the following pairs correctly shows a digestive juice in the area of the alimentary canal where it is produced?

A intestinal juice—stomach
B pancreatic juice—large intestine
C saliva—mouth
D gastric juice—duodenum
E pancreatic juice—ileum

63 Which of the following would make up a balanced diet?

A carbohydrates, fats, proteins, vitamins, mineral salts, water, roughage
B carbohydrates, fats, proteins, vitamins, salt water, fibre
C vitamins, mineral salts, glucose, fats, water, roughage
D vitamins, mineral salts, carbohydrates, no fat, proteins, water, roughage
E sodium chloride, milk, vitamins, carbohydrates, proteins, fat, roughage

EXTENSION QUESTION

64 Which one of the following is **not** the result of malnutrition?

A starvation
B obesity
C rickets
D alcoholism
E hay fever

STRUCTURED QUESTIONS

65 The following is a description of a food test.

> Place a solid piece of food in a test-tube.
> Fill the test-tube with Benedict's solution.
> Heat the test-tube gently for 10 minutes.
> A purple colour indicates the presence of reducing sugar.

The above is incorrect in a number of ways. Make a list of the five mistakes and say what the correct procedure should be.

66 The following diagram illustrates the human digestive system. Indicate which letter(s) give the correct answer to the following statements. Some letters will be used more than once and some letters not at all.

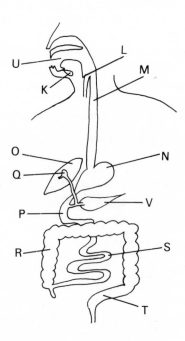

(a) where saliva is produced
(b) where most water is reabsorbed
(c) where the food is churned into a liquid
(d) the structure which prevents choking
(e) where digested products are absorbed
(f) where bile is produced
(g) where bile is stored
(h) where carbohydrates are digested
(i) where fats are digested
(j) where faeces are stored before being voided from the body.

67 The pie chart below gives an indication of the length of time (over a 24 hour period) spent by food in each region of the alimentary canal.

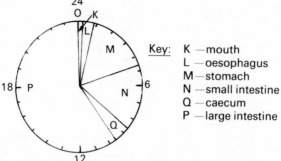

Key: K —mouth
L —oesophagus
M—stomach
N —small intestine
Q —caecum
P —large intestine

(a) Why does food remain in the mouth for such a short time?

(b) For how long does food remain in the small intestine?

(c) Suggest two processes which might be happening during this time.

(d) In which region of the alimentary canal does food spend most time?

(e) Suggest a possible explanation for your answer to **(d)**.

68 In the following five pairs of statements, one or both statements may be correct, and the second statement may be an explanation of the first. Use the letters **A–E** below to give an answer to each of the five pairs of statements.

A both correct, second explains the first
B both correct, second *does not* explain the first
C first correct, second false
D first false, second correct
E both false

First statement	**Second statement**
(a) Lipase is an enzyme which breaks down fats.	Lipase is found in pancreatic juice.
(b) The internal surface of the ileum is covered with villi.	A large surface area is needed for the absorption of food.
(c) The oesophagus does not produce a digestive juice.	The oesophagus is the passage which connects the mouth to the stomach.
(d) The stomach produces a digestive juice which contains no enzymes.	The stomach is a bag in which food remains for some time.
(e) The digested products of fats go directly into capillaries inside the villi.	Villi can only absorb the products of fat digestion.

69 The diagram below shows a model gut. Look at this carefully and answer the questions which follow.

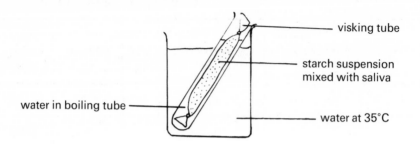

visking tube

starch suspension mixed with saliva

water in boiling tube

water at 35°C

(a) In what way is the visking tubing like the gut wall?
(b) Apart from not being composed of living material, give one way in which the visking tube is different from the gut wall.
(c) If the apparatus was left for 30 minutes and food tests were then carried out on the water in the boiling tube, what results would you expect?
(d) Give a brief explanation of the results.

70 Three jars of commercially-produced baby food were examined and the following information was found on the labels. (Figures all refer to a 100 g sample of the food.)

	Fat	Protein	Carbohydrate	Energy
Apple dessert	2.0 g	1.0 g	12.9 g	290 kJ
Egg custard	3.0 g	2.2 g	15.5 g	395 kJ
Chocolate dessert	2.9 g	3.3 g	16.1 g	415 kJ

(a) Assuming all the jars are sold at the same price and weight, say which one you think is the best value and give your reasons.
(b) Which of the food constituents is especially required in babies' diets and why?
(c) Which baby food do you think contains the most sugar?
(d) Which do you think is richest in dietary fibre?
(e) Which essential components of the diet, apart from water and fibre, are not listed in this information from the labels?

71 The following table gives nutritional information for the items eaten by a man at breakfast.

	Amount eaten /g	Contents per 100 g food			
		Carbohydrate /g	Fat /g	Protein /g	Energy /kJ
Milk	40	5	4	7	280
Cornflakes	20	90	0.5	8	1500
Yoghurt	25	15	2	4	1400
Sugar	5	100	0	0	1600
White coffee	50	0.5	0.5	0	80

(a) What would make up the largest bulk of the milk, apart from the contents listed?

(b) What else would you expect to find in milk which is of nutritional value?

(c) Which food provides the man with the most carbohydrate in this meal?

(d) Which food provides him with the most protein in this meal?

(e) Calculate the total energy intake from this meal.

72 British sailors used to suffer from such disorders as weakness, soft gums, teeth falling out and internal bleeding whilst on extended sea voyages. In 1795 lemon juice was made available to British Navy seamen, and in 1865 this was replaced by lime juice. The symptoms described above are now virtually unknown in the navy.

(a) What disease is characterised by the symptoms described above?

(b) What causes this disease in people?

(c) Explain why taking lemon or lime juice cures the disease.

(d) Name another food that would cure this disease.

It has been found that boiled lime juice is not as effective in alleviating the symptoms as unboiled lime juice.

(e) Why is this?

In very advanced cases of the disease, people are at risk of death and are so weak that they cannot eat or drink.

(f) Suggest how such a patient could be cured today, and explain the reasoning behind your suggested cure.

73 Read the following paragraph carefully before answering the questions which follow.

Children in Saudi Arabia suffer from rickets, a condition caused by vitamin D deficiency. Eighty-four percent of all such children were breast fed. It is customary in Saudi Arabia for women to wear long flowing robes and veils which cover their faces so that only their eyes are exposed to sunlight. An expert said that the high incidence of rickets was due to 'environmental deprivation of sunlight among mothers and their breast fed infants combined with no dietary supplement of vitamin D'.

(a) How does the condition known as rickets affect a person?
(b) What is the relationship between vitamin D and sunlight?
(c) What causes 'environmental deprivation of sunlight'?
(d) Why do you think children who were breast fed are more likely to suffer from rickets than those who were bottle fed?
(e) What is meant by the term 'no dietary supplement'?
(f) Suggest two ways in which the incidence of rickets among Saudi Arabian children could be reduced.

EXTENSION QUESTION

74 The following are some facts about the liver.

Glucose is converted to glycogen.
The hepatic portal vein contains variable amounts of glucose during the day.
The hepatic vein always contains 90 mg glucose per 100 cm³ blood.
Excess amino acids are broken down into urea.
Bile is produced.
The colour of bile is due to the breakdown products of haemoglobin, which is broken down in the liver.
Fat-soluble vitamins are stored in the liver.

Examine the following diagram and use the above information to help you answer the questions.

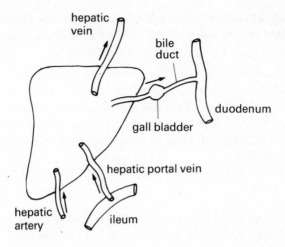

hepatic vein

bile duct

duodenum

gall bladder

hepatic portal vein

hepatic artery

ileum

(a) Why does the hepatic portal vein contain variable amounts of glucose during the day?

(b) Why may bile be regarded as an excretory product?

(c) What is the source of the excess amino acids?

(d) Which blood vessel carries these to the liver?

(e) What happens to the urea formed in the liver?

(f) Why is cod liver oil a good source of vitamins A and D?

(g) Which blood vessel carries oxygenated blood to the liver?

(h) What is the function of the gall bladder?

MULTIPLE CHOICE QUESTIONS

75 Which of the following substances is **not** transported by either xylem or phloem?

A   amino acids
B   glucose
C   nitrates
D   water
E   starch

76 Minerals, absorbed by plant roots, are taken to developing buds high up on the stem. This transport occurs:

A   by the transpiration stream in the xylem
B   by translocation in the xylem
C   by translocation in the phloem
D   by the transpiration stream in the phloem
E   by transpiration in the vascular bundles

D

77 When leaves are tested after a day in the sun they are found to contain lots of starch. However if tested in the morning, they contain no starch. The **best** explanation for this 'destarching' of leaves in the dark is that:

A   the starch has been used up in respiration
B   the starch test does not work in the morning
C   the starch has been transported out of the leaves
D   the starch has been turned to sugar and transported out of the leaves
E   the starch has been turned into protein and stored in the leaves

78 The following diagram illustrates a simple potometer which measures water uptake in plants. Which **one** of the following combinations of conditions would result in the fastest uptake of water?

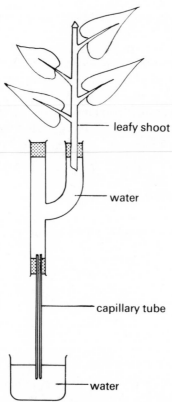

leafy shoot

water

capillary tube

water

A   bright light and humid air
B   moving air (i.e. in a breeze) and low temperature
C   high temperature and bright light
D   still air and dim light
E   high humidity and high temperature

79   The xylem and phloem transport substances through plants.
     Which of the following statements describes this process best?

A   the xylem transports water upwards, the phloem transports
     food downwards
B   the xylem transports water and salts, the phloem transports
     soluble food substances
C   the xylem transports water and salts upwards, the phloem
     transports soluble food substances upwards and downwards
D   the xylem transports soluble food substances upwards, the
     phloem transports water and salts downwards
E   the xylem transports water and salts downwards, the phloem
     transports soluble food substances upwards

STRUCTURED QUESTIONS

80   Examine the diagrams below and then answer the following
questions.

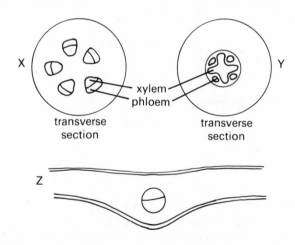

(a) What two substances are carried by the xylem?
(b) Name one other substance carried by the phloem.
(c) Which of the two diagrams, X or Y, shows a stem?
(d) Give one reason for your answer to (c).
(e) A plant is put in a beaker containing a pink dye and allowed
     to sit for twenty-four hours. Sections are then cut off the stem.
     Which part of the stem would show the pink dye?
(f) Z is a diagram of a section through a leaf. Copy this out and
     label the xylem and phloem.
(g) What are vascular bundles in leaves more usually called?

81 The diagram below represents a potometer. Three of these were set up and labelled X, Y and Z. Use the following key to answer the questions.

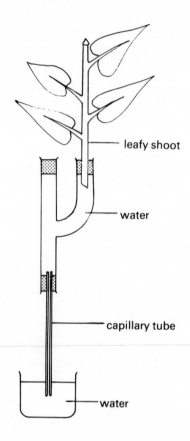

- leafy shoot
- water
- capillary tube
- water

potometer X—placed near a sunny window
potometer Y—placed in a dark room
potometer Z—all the leaves were covered with Vaseline and
  the apparatus was placed near a sunny window

(a) Which apparatus is the control?
(b) What hypothesis are X and Y testing?
(c) What other difference might there be between the surroundings of X and Y which might affect the experiment?
(d) How would you set up an experiment to find out if this condition did affect the results?
(e) In which potometer would the rate of water loss be the greatest?

82 The diagram below shows a type of potometer which may be used to demonstrate transpiration.

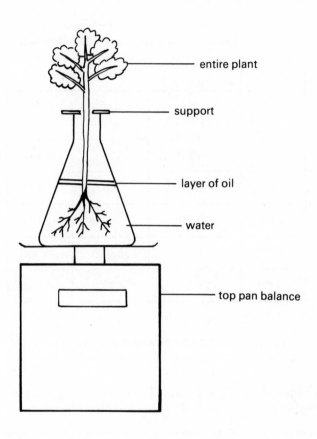

(a) What precaution(s) would you take in setting up this apparatus?

(b) How can this apparatus be used to measure transpiration?

(c) Describe how the apparatus could be used to investigate the influence of one named environmental factor.

(d) Outline briefly the kind of results you might expect when investigating this environmental factor.

(e) How would you attempt to show the passage of water through the plant?

83 In an investigation of the mineral salts taken up by the roots of plants, some soil and the plants growing in it were chemically analysed after drying in an oven at 60 °C.
Table I below shows the results obtained.

| Element tested for | Mass of element in mg/100 g dry mass | | | | |
| | | Plant species | | | |
	Soil	Knapweed	Birdsfoot trefoil	Salad burnet	Sedge
N	0.95	1970.0	2650.0	1900.0	1570.0
P	0.16	107.0	89.0	110.0	110.0
K	10.8	1730.0	1200.0	1030.0	1470.0
Ca	928.3	2400.0	3530.0	2870.0	750.0
Mg	18.0	260.0	230.0	520.0	150.0

Table I

(N = nitrogen, P = phosphorus, K = potassium, Ca = calcium, Mg = magnesium)

(a) Use the information in Table I to complete Table II to show the abundance of each element in each material.

	Order of abundance most⟶least				
Soil					
Knapweed					
Birdsfoot trefoil					
Salad burnet					
Sedge					

Table II

(b) Why was it necessary to dry the soil and plant material before analysing it?

(c) Using Table I, what can you say in general about the concentration of the elements tested in plant material and in the surrounding soil?

(d) Using Table II, which element is:

    (i) more abundant in plant material than in soil?

    (ii) less abundant in plant material than in soil?

    (iii) equally abundant in plant material and in soil?

84 In an experiment to investigate the role of the phloem in translocation, the leaves of two young saplings were kept in an atmosphere containing radioactive carbon dioxide ($^{14}CO_2$). Phloem tissue was killed by treating with steam and the movement of soluble food substances was subsequently traced using a Geiger Müller tube (which detects radioactivity).

The results are summarised diagrammatically below.

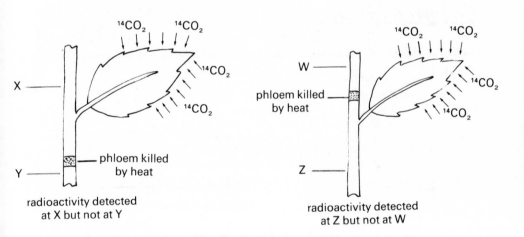

Now answer the following questions.

(a) Why is steam an effective method of killing phloem tissue?

(b) Why is steam treatment preferable to removal of the bark?

(c) Briefly explain the relationship between the radioactive carbon dioxide and the radioactivity detected at X.

(d) What is the significance of these results in terms of:

    (i) the direction of movement of soluble food substances in plants?

    (ii) the tissue in which soluble food substances are transported?

85   In the light, green plants make carbohydrates in their leaves and
      transport them to other parts of the plant. Two such foods
      commonly found in plants are starch and sugar. Starch is tasteless
      and insoluble. Sugar is sweet-tasting and soluble. Use the above
      information to explain the following observations.

      (a) Leaves of sweet vernal grass taken from a field on a sunny day
      are tasteless when chewed.
      (b) Stems from the same plant are sweet when chewed.
      (c) Washed roots from the same plant are tasteless when chewed.
      (d) Leaves of sweet vernal grass tested for starch and sugar after
      being kept in the dark for several hours contained neither
      carbohydrate.
      (e) Sheep gain most nourishment from grass when grazing in the
      afternoon.

MULTIPLE CHOICE QUESTIONS

86   Which of the following is **not** transported in blood plasma?

      A   hormones
      B   oxygen
      C   carbon dioxide
      D   glucose
      E   urea

87   Blood leaves the heart in two vessels. These are:

      A   the pulmonary artery and pulmonary vein
      B   the aorta and the vena cava
      C   the vena cava and pulmonary artery
      D   the pulmonary vein and aorta
      E   the pulmonary artery and aorta

88   The hepatic portal vein carries blood:

      A   from the liver to the heart
      B   from the alimentary canal to the pancreas
      C   from the alimentary canal to the liver
      D   from the liver to the alimentary canal
      E   from the alimentary canal to the heart

89 The diagram below shows a small section of vein where one vein is joining another. Three semi-lunar valves are shown. Which of the following best describes the direction in which venous blood flows?

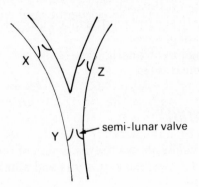

semi-lunar valve

A from X to Y and from Y to Z
B from Z to X and from Y to X
C from Y to X and from Y to Z
D from X to Z and from Y to Z
E from Z to X and from Z to Y

90 Which of the following would you consider to be **bad** advice for preventing coronary heart disease?

A don't smoke
B have your blood pressure checked regularly
C maintain ideal body weight
D eat plenty of saturated fats
E find a way of relaxing to reduce stress

91 When referring to what happens when the left ventricle contracts, which of the following is **not** true?

A the right ventricle contracts
B the blood passes into the aorta
C the semi-lunar valve in the aorta opens
D a pulse is produced in arteries
E the bicuspid valve opens

EXTENSION QUESTION

92 Which one of the following is **not** a function of the lymphatic system?

    A   transport of fatty acids
    B   returning tissue fluid to the blood stream
    C   transport of glycerol
    D   defence against bacteria
    E   bathing the tissues

STRUCTURED QUESTIONS

93 The diagram below shows the main plan of the blood circulatory system in man. Using the key letters and numbers, answer the following questions.

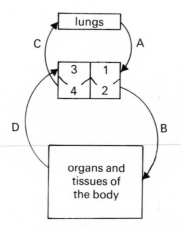

(a) Which letters represent arteries?
(b) Which letters represent blood vessels carrying oxygenated blood?
(c) In which blood vessel is the pressure highest?
(d) What is the advantage of having four chambers in the heart?
(e) List those parts of the body, represented on the diagram, where capillaries are found.
(f) List those parts of the body, represented on the diagram, where exchange of materials takes place by diffusion.
(g) Suggest one waste product carried by the blood which would be found mostly in chambers 3 and 4.
(h) Suggest one waste product carried by the blood which would be present equally in all four chambers.
(i) Why is this system sometimes called a 'double circulatory system'?

94 The following is a diagram of part of the blood system.

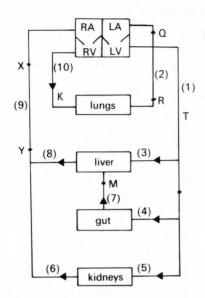

RA = right atrium (auricle)
RV = right ventricle
LA = left atrium (auricle)
LV = left ventricle

Here is some information about the blood system.

Blood travelling in arteries normally carries oxygenated blood.
Blood travelling in veins normally carries deoxygenated blood.
Blood receives oxygen when it travels through the lungs.
Blood flows away from the heart in arteries.
Blood flows towards the heart in veins.

Now answer the following questions, using the numbers given on the diagram where necessary.

(a) Which blood vessels are arteries?
(b) Does blood entering the heart do so through the atria or ventricles?
(c) Which blood vessels are veins?
(d) Which organ has two blood supplies: lungs, liver, gut or kidneys?
(e) Which side of the heart contains oxygenated blood?
(f) What is unusual about vessel number 2?
(g) In what direction is blood flowing between:
   (i) Q and R?
   (ii) X and Y?
(h) What type of blood is to be found at:
   (i) K?
   (ii) T?
   (iii) X?

95 The following information was collected by a class of eleven year olds.

Name	Heart beat per min
Mary	72
John	70
Martha	74
Annabel	76
Rachel	78
James	70
Timothy	68
Jane	72

Name	Heart beat per min
Matthew	70
Joan	78
Ivan	71
Alan	69
Ian	70
Clare	76
Anne	74
Frank	72

(a) Rearrange these results so that there is one table for girls and one for boys.

(b) Work out the average heart beat for the girls group by adding up their heart beats and dividing by eight. Show your working.

(c) Work out the average heart beat for the boys in the same way.

(d) Which group has the higher heart beat rate?

The class then went to PE. Each person in the class had to run 800 metres and their heart beat was recorded when they returned. The results are shown in the following tables (on facing page).

(e) Whose heart beat increased the most?

(f) Whose heart beat increased the least?

(g) What is the advantage of the increase in heart beat during exercise?

Name	Heart beat per min		Name	Heart beat per min
Mary	120		Matthew	116
John	120		Joan	126
Martha	126		Ivan	112
Annabel	126		Alan	114
Rachel	128		Ian	117
James	120		Clare	120
Timothy	110		Anne	118
Jane	120		Frank	121

96 Read the following lines carefully.

> *A red blood corpuscle once said:*
> *'In ninety days time I'll be dead,*
> *My life's been in vein*
> *I should start it again*
> *And be a white blood cell instead'.*

(a) Explain the biology behind the phrase 'In ninety days time I'll be dead, . . .'.

(b) Where in the body are red blood cells manufactured?

(c) What is the function of a red blood cell?

(d) What happens to red blood cells when they die and in which organ of the body does this occur?

(e) State two differences between red blood corpuscles and white blood corpuscles.

(f) What is biologically incorrect about the statement 'My life's been in vein . . .'?

97 The following diagram shows a human heart in longitudinal section.

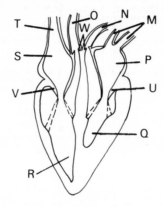

(a) Which letters indicate the ventricles?
(b) Which letters indicate veins?
(c) Which letters indicate valves?
(d) Which side of the heart carries deoxygenated blood?
(e) Why would vessels M and O be short?
(f) Which ventricle has the thicker wall?
(g) In which ventricle would there be greater pressure?
(h) Why is this necessary?
(i) In what position is U:
　(i)　when the heart is filling with blood?
　(ii)　when the heart is contracting?
(j) Which valves are open when the ventricles are contracting?
(k) By reference to the relevant structures, explain how blood enters from vessel M, passes through the heart, and leaves from vessel N.

98 The heart muscle's blood is supplied by the coronary arteries, which arise near the start of the aorta and penetrate into the ventricle walls.

(a) What useful materials are delivered to the walls of the ventricles by the coronary arteries?
(b) Why is the blood passing through the heart not able to supply these materials directly?
(c) What would happen to the volume of blood being supplied by the coronary arteries during a period of vigorous exercise?
(d) If a capillary arising from a coronary artery became blocked, what would be the effect on the muscle cells that it would normally supply?
(e) Give three reasons why blockage of a larger branch of a coronary artery may cause death.

99 Look at the table showing percentage deaths from coronary heart disease for males and females at different ages in 1978.

Age group	25–34	35–44	45–54	55–64	65–74	All ages
Males	6%	29%	41%	39%	34%	32
Females	3%	8%	13%	21%	28%	24

Indicate whether the following statements are true or false.

(a) Twice as many men as women die from coronary heart disease.

(b) The most dangerous age for coronary heart disease is 45–54 years for men.

(c) Sixty per cent of men and women die from coronary heart disease between 65–74 years.

(d) The ratio of male to female deaths for all ages is 4 : 3.

(e) Women are less prone to die from coronary heart disease at all ages.

100 The following graph shows the blood pressure in the aorta and the left ventricle throughout one heart beat.

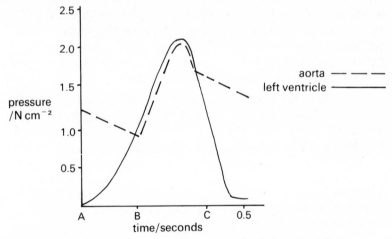

(a) What is the maximum pressure in the left ventricle?

(b) What is the minimum pressure in the aorta?

(c) How many times would the heart pump blood out in one minute?

(d) During which part of the cycle is the pressure in the left ventricle higher than that in the aorta?

(e) At what point on the graph does the valve between the left ventricle and the aorta open so that blood flows from the heart into the aorta?

(f) At what point on the graph does the valve between the left ventricle and the aorta close?

EXTENSION QUESTION

101 The diagram below is based on observations made by William Harvey, a physician who lived in the 17th century.

(a) The swellings shown on the blood vessels in the diagram are valves. In what kind of blood vessels are they found?

(b) Figure B shows the appearance of a blood vessel which has been firmly stroked in the direction shown. Explain the apparent disappearance of the blood vessel.

(c) What would you expect to happen if the fingertip pressure was removed?

(d) What does Harvey's demonstration show?

About 100 years later, the Reverend Stephen Hales carried out investigations on the circulatory system of plants. On one occasion, he attempted to stop the flow of sap (water and salts) from the broken stem of an old vine by tying a piece of bladder over the end. After a couple of days, the bladder had become swollen with sap. By replacing the bladder with a tight-fitting tube he found that sap rose up the tube.

(e) Using the terms *soil water*, *cell sap*, *osmosis* and *root hairs*, explain how the liquid reached the broken end of the vine stem.

(f) What does the swelling of the bladder, or the upward movement of the liquid, tell you about the *pressure* involved?

(g) In the unbroken stems of a vine, water would also be moving in an upward direction. Why?

(h) Give one difference between the flow of blood in an animal and the flow of liquid in a plant.

MULTIPLE CHOICE QUESTIONS

102 Which of the following is **not** a characteristic of a respiratory surface, such as lungs or gills?

A moist
B thick
C large surface area
D efficient blood supply
E efficient air supply

103 The best description of gas exchange in the lungs is:

A   passage of carbon dioxide into the alveoli
B   passage of oxygen into the alveoli and carbon dioxide into the blood
C   passage of oxygen into the blood and carbon dioxide into the alveoli
D   passage of oxygen into and out of the blood only
E   passage of nitrogen into the blood

104 Which one of the following diagrams correctly shows how two boiling tubes and a T-shaped glass tube can be connected to demonstrate the effect of inhaled and exhaled air on an indicator solution?

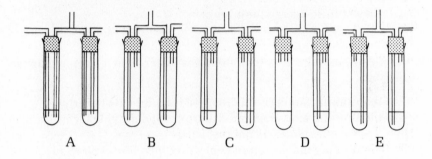

105 In a gas analysis experiment using a J-tube, the following results were obtained.

Original length of air bubble	100 mm
Length after adding potassium hydroxide (KOH) solution	99 mm
Length after adding pyrogallol	84 mm

Which of the following statements correctly gives the percentage of oxygen and carbon dioxide in the air sample?

A   0.1% CO_2 and 1.6% O_2
B   1% CO_2 and 16% O_2
C   16% CO_2 and 1% O_2
D   1% CO_2 and 15% O_2
E   15% CO_2 and 1% O_2

106 Which of the following is the best definition of respiration?

A   exchange of gases at a respiratory surface
B   release of energy from food
C   production of energy from food
D   using up oxygen in the body and producing carbon dioxide
E   carrying oxygen to where it can be used by cells

107 Which of the following statements about the site of respiration is **not** true?

A it occurs in living cells
B it occurs in the hair of mammals
C it occurs in the green cells of plants
D it occurs in the muscle cells of animals
E it occurs in microbes

108 Germinating seeds have a high rate of respiration because:

A they photosynthesise a lot
B they require carbon dioxide for cell division
C they require light for photosynthesis
D they photosynthesise very little
E they require energy for growth

109 A mouse running a treadmill breathes faster than a sleeping mouse because:

A the running mouse requires more food for extra energy
B the running mouse requires more carbon dioxide for its cells
C the sleeping mouse is not respiring
D the running mouse requires more oxygen for respiration
E the sleeping mouses loses no heat energy

110 Which one of the following is **not** caused by smoking?

A lung cancer
B high blood pressure
C carbon monoxide poisoning
D bronchitis
E diabetes

111 Which one of the following statements about smoking has been confirmed as true:

A chemicals from tobacco can be carcinogenic
B filter-tip cigarettes are harmless
C no harmful chemicals are found in pipe tobacco
D the chance of dying younger is reduced by smoking
E it does no harm to smoke a few cigarettes a day when you are young and healthy

EXTENSION QUESTION

112 The following diagram shows appropriate apparatus which investigates the breathing of woodlice. Which one of the following statements **best** describes what will be observed?

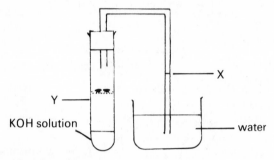

A   level X will go down
B   level Y will go up
C   both X and Y will stay the same
D   level X will go up
E   level Y will go down

STRUCTURED QUESTIONS

113 Five volunteers were used in an experiment in which their breathing rates were measured at rest and after running 300 m. Here are the results.

	Breathing rate (breaths per minute)	
Subject	at rest	after exercise
A	10	29
B	18	32
C	14	27
D	19	32
E	9	24

(a) Display this data on graph paper using the histogram technique to show clearly the effects of exercise on the individuals.
(b) What is it about exercise that causes these changes in breathing rate to occur?
(c) Calculate the percentage increase in breathing rate for subject A.

(d) All the subjects ran the same distance. Does this prove that those showing the greatest increase in the breathing rate are less fit than the others?

(e) Explain your answer to **(d)**.

114 Look carefully at the diagram below, showing gas exchange in an alveolus (air sac), and answer the questions which follow.

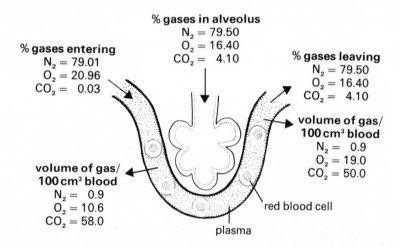

% gases in alveolus
N_2 = 79.50
O_2 = 16.40
CO_2 = 4.10

% gases entering
N_2 = 79.01
O_2 = 20.96
CO_2 = 0.03

% gases leaving
N_2 = 79.50
O_2 = 16.40
CO_2 = 4.10

volume of gas/ 100 cm³ blood
N_2 = 0.9
O_2 = 19.0
CO_2 = 50.0

volume of gas/ 100 cm³ blood
N_2 = 0.9
O_2 = 10.6
CO_2 = 58.0

red blood cell

plasma

(a) Account for the change in the level of oxygen entering and leaving the lungs.

(b) Account for the change in the level of carbon dioxide entering and leaving the lungs.

(c) What happens to the nitrogen in the lungs?

(d) What special feature of red blood cells allows them to carry oxygen?

(e) Why does panting take place while running in a race?

(f) What would happen to the red blood cells if some carbon monoxide was inhaled?

(g) How might this be compensated?

(h) Why would artificial resuscitation be of little use to someone who had been overcome by carbon monoxide and whose breathing had stopped?

(i) How may people who normally live at high altitude overcome the smaller volume of oxygen in the atmosphere?

(j) What advantage may this be to an athlete who lives at high altitude but competes at low altitude?

115 In the following experiment several tubes containing some bicarbonate indicator solution (B/I) were used in conjunction with a water plant and/or a small invertebrate animal. The tubes were set up as shown in the diagram below.

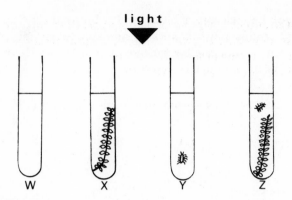

light

W   X   Y   Z

The B/I solution was orange at the beginning of the experiment.

(a) What colour would the B/I solution be in tubes W, X and Y at the end of 1 hour?

(b) Explain your answer for tube X.

(c) Which tube was the control?

(d) What process is going on in tube Y?

(e) How would you explain the colour of the B/I solution in tube Z if it remained orange?

116 Look carefully at these diagrams which illustrate the beginning and end of a biological experiment, then attempt to answer the questions which follow.

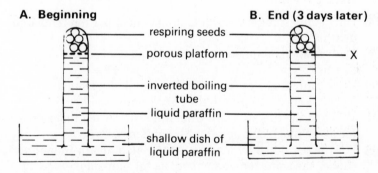

A. Beginning   **B. End (3 days later)**

respiring seeds

porous platform ——————— X

inverted boiling
tube

liquid paraffin

shallow dish of
liquid paraffin

(a) Why does the liquid paraffin not run out of the boiling tube in diagram A?

(b) How would you treat the seeds before putting them into this apparatus to ensure that they will be alive and respiring?

(c) Why do you think it is preferable to use liquid paraffin in this experiment, rather than water?

(d) Old text books use mercury in this experiment, instead of liquid paraffin. Why is mercury not recommended now?

(e) What do you expect to be in space X?

(f) Explain your answer to **(e)**.

117 The graph below compares the level of lung cancer deaths in three different groups: non-smokers (o), smokers (●) and people who have given up smoking for various periods (------). Using the graph, answer the questions which follow.

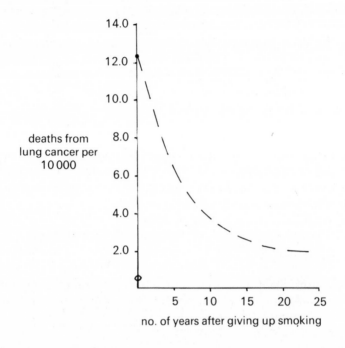

deaths from lung cancer per 10 000

no. of years after giving up smoking

(a) How many smokers die from lung cancer per ten thousand deaths?

(b) How many non-smokers die from lung cancer per ten thousand deaths?

(c) How many times greater is the risk of death from lung cancer for smokers compared to the risk for non-smokers?

(d) When is the risk of death from lung cancer ten times greater for ex-smokers compared with non-smokers?

(e) For the period shown, when is the risk of death from lung cancer the same for ex-smokers as for non-smokers?

118 The following diagram shows a model breathing apparatus.

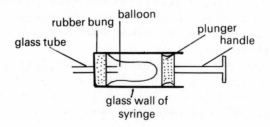

(a) To which part of the human body are the following equivalent.
- (i) glass tube
- (ii) balloon
- (iii) glass wall of syringe
- (iv) plunger

(b) Consider what happens when the plunger handle is pulled out.
- (i) What happens to the volume in the syringe (outside the balloon)?
- (ii) What happens to the pressure?
- (iii) Does air move into or out of the balloon?
- (iv) Explain exactly why air moves in this direction.

The iron lung shown below is an artificial aid to breathing. It is used by patients who can no longer breathe, e.g. when a disease like polio has paralysed the intercostal muscles. The machine works in exactly the same way as the 'syringe model' in part **(a)** of this question.

iron lung

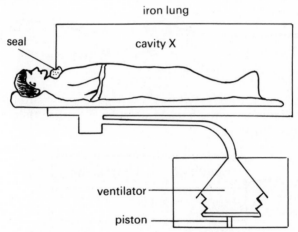

(c)
- (i) What happens to the pressure in the chamber of the iron lung (labelled X) when the piston of the ventilator moves upwards?
- (ii) How will this affect the air in the lungs of the patient?
- (iii) What will happen to the pressure in chamber X when the ventilator piston moves down?
- (iv) Explain whether this will bring about inhalation or exhalation in the patient.
- (v) Why is it essential to have a good seal round the patient's neck?
- (vi) Can paralysed patients leave the iron lung for any length of time? Explain your answer.
- (vii) Describe two difficulties which might be experienced by a patient who must live permanently in an iron lung.

119 A pupil is investigating the effect of certain substances on animal muscle. The muscle used in the experiment was obtained by tearing out long strands of freshly butchered steak.

The strand of muscle selected was first measured dry, and then soaked in water and remeasured. The water was dried off and a solution of glucose applied. After one minute, the length of muscle strand was measured again. The excess glucose was dried off and a few drops of ATP solution were added. (*ATP is a chemical found in cells which provides them with large quantities of energy.*) One minute elapsed before the muscle strand was measured again. The drawings below show the results obtained.

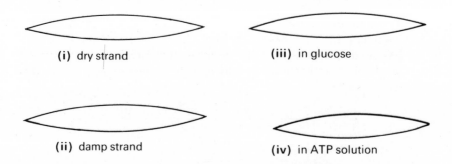

(i) dry strand

(iii) in glucose

(ii) damp strand

(iv) in ATP solution

(a) Copy out the table below. Then use a ruler to carefully measure the diagrams of the muscle strands. Complete the table with your results.

Condition	Length/mm
dry	
damp	
glucose	
ATP	

(b) Now explain the following.
  (i) Any change in length between (i) and (ii).
  (ii) Any change in length between (iii) and (iv).
(c) What is the percentage change in length between (iii) and (iv)?
(d) What is the reason for the large change between (iii) and (iv)?

EXTENSION QUESTION

120 Look at these figures, which show the approximate O_2 requirements of winning Olympic athletes.

Event	Top speed /kmph	Oxygen needed during event /dm³	Oxygen breathed in during event /dm³
100 m	37	10	0.5
1500 m	25	36	19
10 000 m	21.5	150	133

The oxygen debt of an athlete is the volume of oxygen that he or she needs to take in after the event to make up for the amount that was needed during the event.

(a) Calculate the O_2 debt for the three races.
(b) What is the relationship between the length of the race and the top speed of the runner?
(c) What is the relationship between the length of the race and the oxygen needed?
(d) What do you think is the maximum O_2 debt?
(e) Give a reason for your answer to (d).
(f) What type of respiration was used to provide energy during the build up of the oxygen debt?

MULTIPLE CHOICE QUESTIONS

121 When a plant grows in a curved shape in response to the direction of light in the environment, this is known as:

A active transport
B transpiration
C translocation
D transplantation
E phototropism

122 A tropism is shown by:

    A   a snail retracting into its shell when touched
    B   a geranium plant bending towards the light
    C   the leaves falling off an ash tree in autumn
    D   a daisy opening its petals in the early morning sun
    E   a lizard going into the shade on a very hot day

STRUCTURED QUESTIONS

123 Consider the following information.

Phototropism is a growth response to light.
Shoots are positively phototropic, i.e. they grow towards light.
The chemical in plants which is responsible for this tropism is
called an auxin.
Auxin promotes cell enlargement (growth).
Auxin is produced in the tips of stems.
Auxin is destroyed by light, or moves away from that part of the
plant exposed to light.

Now answer the following questions.

(a) Why do pot plants placed on a window sill grow towards the
window?
(b) Why do people who look after their pot plants well turn them
round regularly?
(c) Why do plants kept in the dark grow taller than plants kept in
the light?
(d) The following diagram illustrates an experiment on the growth
of very young shoots.

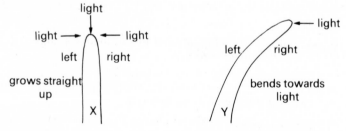

  (i) What can you say about the amount of auxin on all sides
in X?
  (ii) What can you say about the amount of auxin on the left
and right hand sides of Y?
  (iii) What can you say about the amount of growth there will
be on the left and right hand sides of Y?
  (iv) Explain concisely why plants grow towards the light.

EXTENSION QUESTION

124 Geotropism is a growth movement of a plant in response to gravity. Stems are *negatively* geotropic and roots are *positively* geotropic. Examine the diagram below which shows three stages in the life of a poppy.

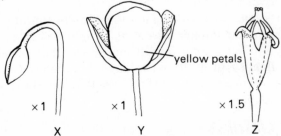

(a) Which stage or stages show positive geotropism?
(b) Which stage or stages show negative geotropism?
(c) What is the advantage of geotropism to the bud and flower?
(d) Think about the way in which poppy seeds are dispersed and explain why the seed capsule is carried on a long stem and why it demonstrates the type of geotropism that it does.

MULTIPLE CHOICE QUESTIONS

125 A receptor has to be:
    A a complicated organ, like the eye
    B made up of at least one sensory cell
    C a group of motor cells
    D within the spinal cord
    E in the head region of the body

126 Which one of the following is **not** true of the skin?
    A it always has hairs
    B it protects the body against mechanical damage
    C it is sensitive to touch
    D it helps to control body temperature
    E it helps to retain water

127 When light enters the eye, it passes through various regions until it reaches the optic nerve. Which of the following gives the correct order for light passing through the eye?
    A pupil, cornea, lens, retina
    B lens, pupil, retina, cornea
    C cornea, lens, pupil, retina
    D cornea, pupil, lens, retina
    E lens, cornea, pupil, retina

128 The largest species of deer in the world is the elk or moose of northern Canada and Alaska. The smallest species of deer in the world is the pudu of tropical Equador. Which one of the following statements is most likely to be true?

   A   the elk has a smaller surface area than the pudu
   B   the pudu has thicker insulation than the elk
   C   the pudu has proportionally longer ears than the elk
   D   the elk has a proportionally longer tail than the pudu
   E   the pudu has a larger surface area than the elk

STRUCTURED QUESTIONS

129 Examine the following section through an eye.

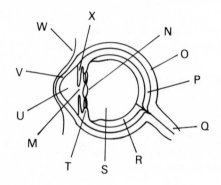

(a) Name parts M–X.
(b) Which part:
    (i) carries nerve impulses to the brain?
    (ii) helps to give the eye its shape?
    (iii) controls the amount of light entering the eye?
    (iv) lines the inside of the eyelid?
    (v) mainly focuses the light?
    (vi) prevents reflection within the eye?
    (vii) has muscles attached to it for moving the eye?
(c) The clear covering at the front of the eye is a living tissue but it contains no capillaries. How is oxygen supplied to this tissue?

130 The following diagram illustrates the iris and the pupil of an eye.

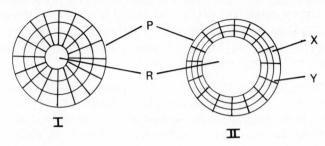

(a) What is P?

(b) What is R?

(c) Measure the diameter of R in each diagram.

(d) Which eye is in dim light?

(e) In this eye, say which muscles in P are contracted: the circular muscles or the radial muscles?

(f) In II which type of muscle is illustrated by:
  (i) X?
  (ii) Y?

131

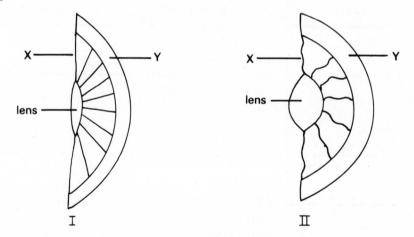

(a) In the above diagram, which lens is adapted for looking at things:
  (i) far away?
  (ii) near?

(b) What are X and Y?

(c) What state is X in, in diagram I?

(d) What state is Y in, in diagram II?

(e) Why does the state described in (d) above allow the lens to be fat?

(f) Why is this state tiring?

132 The Polar bear is a native of the Arctic. It is one of the largest of the bear family and has a thick white coat and a thick layer of body fat. The Malay bear is only about one quarter of the size of the Polar bear and has a finer coat and much less body fat. It comes from south-east Asia. Are the following statements true or false?

(a) The Malay bear has a larger surface area than the Polar bear.

(b) The Polar bear has a larger volume than the Malay bear.

(c) The Polar bear is insulated better than the Malay bear.

(d) The Malay bear has a smaller surface area to volume ratio than the Polar bear.

In order to maintain a constant body temperature, many animals can make adjustments to either conserve heat and keep warm when the environment is too cold, or to lose heat more quickly and cool down when the environment is too hot.

(e) Copy out the following table and fill in the blank spaces using appropriate words to describe five common adjustments that animals may use to control their temperature.

Name	Description	Effect
	evaporation of water from the skin	
	blood vessels in the skin open wider, more blood at body surface, skin goes red	
vasoconstriction		heat lost more slowly
	rapid reflex contraction of the muscles	

EXTENSION QUESTION

133 Animals take in energy in the form of food and lose energy in various ways, often in the form of heat. Dogs have few or no sweat glands in their skin but pant in hot weather. Humming birds are very small and some reduce their temperature to that of the environment every night, i.e. they 'hibernate' overnight, every night.

(a) How do animals normally take in energy?
(b) By what process is energy released in animals and where does this occur?
(c) What would happen to the temperature of an animal if it lost more energy than it could take in?
(d) Explain how panting helps dogs in hot weather.
(e) Why are humming birds particularly at risk during cold periods?
(f) How does this overnight behaviour help them to survive?

MULTIPLE CHOICE QUESTIONS

134 Which one of the following is **not** a reflex action?

   A   chewing
   B   sneezing
   C   yawning
   D   blinking
   E   coughing

135 The following is a diagram of a sensory neuron (nerve cell).

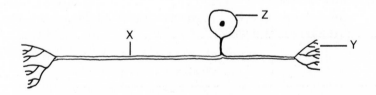

Which of the following is the correct sequence for impulses passing through the cell?

A X, Y, Z   B Z, Y, X   C X, Z, Y   D Y, X, Z   E Y, Z, X

136 When a finger is damaged by a sharp object, the nervous system causes the finger to be quickly withdrawn.

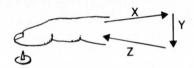

What sequence of nerves is represented by the arrows labelled X, Y and Z?

	X	Y	Z
A	sensory neuron	motor neuron	association neuron
B	association neuron	sensory neuron	motor neuron
C	association neuron	motor neuron	sensory neuron
D	motor neuron	association neuron	sensory neuron
E	sensory neuron	association neuron	motor neuron

EXTENSION QUESTION

137 The trigeminal nerve is the fifth cranial nerve of vertebrates and connects the brain with the teeth and with the skin of the face. Knowing that when the dentist administers a local anaesthetic by injection you can no longer feel pain and you cannot smile properly, you can now conclude that:

A the trigeminal nerve carries reflex messages
B the trigeminal nerve contains mainly motor fibres
C the trigeminal nerve contains mainly sensory fibres
D the trigeminal nerve contains both motor and sensory fibres
E the trigeminal nerve carries messages from the brain to the teeth and back again

138 The following diagram shows the same choice chamber, viewed from above, throughout the course of an experiment. The positions of five woodlice are shown at successive two minute intervals.

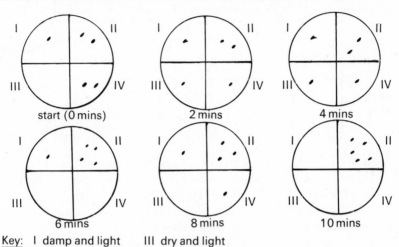

Key: I damp and light III dry and light
      II damp and dark IV dry and dark

(a) Copy out the following table and record the results shown by the diagram.

Condition	Start	2 mins	4 mins	6 mins	8 mins	10 mins	Total sightings
I							
II							
III							
IV							

(b) Why do the numbers of woodlice in the different parts of the choice chamber change during the course of the experiment?

(c) Which of the following statements, based on these results, are true or false?
  (i) Woodlice prefer dry conditions, rather than damp.
  (ii) Woodlice prefer dark conditions, rather than light.
  (iii) Woodlice prefer dry/light to damp/light conditions.
  (iv) Woodlice prefer damp/light to damp/dark conditions.

(d) Use the results to explain your answers to part **(c)** above.

(e) From the results of this experiment, in what kind of conditions might you expect woodlice to be found?

E

139 In an experiment to find out what temperature woodlice prefer, a special type of choice chamber was used. This chamber is illustrated below.

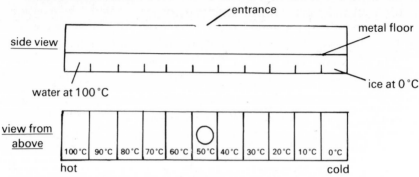

Notice that this choice chamber is rectangular, not circular. Twenty woodlice were introduced into the apparatus after it had stood ready for half an hour. Half an hour later, the number of woodlice at different points along the floor were counted. The results are shown in the table below.

Approximate temperature /°C	Number of woodlice
0	2
10	6
20	8
30	3
40	1
50	0
60	0
70	0
80	0
90	0
100	0

(a) Construct a bar chart of these results.

(b) Why was a metal floor used in the apparatus?

(c) Why was the choice chamber not circular?

(d) Which temperature do woodlice prefer?

140 The following diagram represents the stages in the operation of a simple spinal reflex.

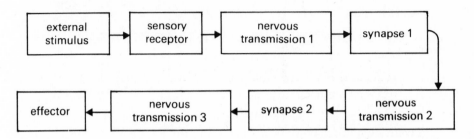

For the knee-jerk reflex, answer the following questions using the above diagram to help you.

(a) Describe the nature of the external stimulus.

(b) Where and what is the sensory receptor?

(c) What type of nerve cell (neuron) is responsible for nervous transmission 1?

(d) Where is the nerve cell that performs nervous transmission 2?

(e) What type of nerve cell is responsible for nervous transmission 3?

(f) Where is synapse 1?

(g) Where is synapse 2?

(h) What is the nature of the effector?

(i) Describe the effect of the reflex.

EXTENSION QUESTION

141 If the sole of a young infant's foot is gently stroked, the toes curl downwards and then quickly turn upwards. This is known as the Babinski response and can be used as a medical test for babies.

(a) What type of action or movement is shown by the Babinski response?

(b) What bodily sense is detecting the stimulus in this case?

(c) Where are the sensory cells located?

(d) What major system of the body is being tested by this method?

(e) What test is traditionally applied to adults when this major bodily system is being examined?

(f) Give one reason why this test is not usually given to babies.

MULTIPLE CHOICE QUESTIONS

142 Which one of the following is **not** an effector organ?

A   skeletal muscle
B   the eye
C   adrenal gland
D   salivary gland
E   iris

143 Which one of the following best describes the function of a ligament?

A   attaches a bone to a muscle
B   attaches a muscle to a muscle
C   attaches a bone to a tendon
D   attaches a bone to a bone
E   attaches cartilage to a bone

144 In which one of the following are both structures examples of effector organs?

A   muscles and bones
B   ligaments and tendons
C   muscles and glands
D   glands and secretions
E   bones and glands

EXTENSION QUESTION

145 An 'effector' is described as a structure of the body which carries out the responses of the organism. Effectors, therefore, are cells, glands, muscles or organs which *act* or *do* things for the individual. Which one of the following organs can be described principally as an effector?

A   a premolar
B   the lungs
C   an eye
D   the bicuspid valve
E   the gall bladder

STRUCTURED QUESTIONS

146 Examine the following diagram which shows the elbow joint in man.

(a) Name the structures M, R, S, T and W.
(b) What is the function of the tendon?

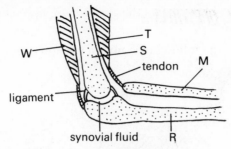

(c) What is the function of the ligament?

(d) What is the function of the synovial fluid?

(e) Ligaments stretch but tendons do not. How is this fact related to the separate functions of these structures?

(f) Why would it be a disadvantage if tendons were elastic?

147 Examine the following diagram.

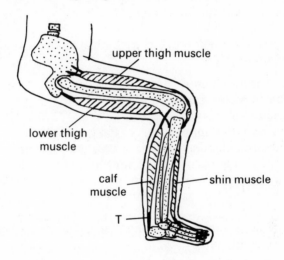

(a) Which muscle must contract to straighten the leg from the position shown?

(b) Which muscle must then contract to bring the leg back to this position again?

(c) What is the name given to a pair of muscles which act together in this way?

(d) Which muscle must contract to move the toes downwards?

(e) Which muscle must contract to bring the toes back up?

(f) Which two muscles in the diagram are acting as extensors?

(g) In walking, the shin muscle and the calf muscle are very important. Thinking carefully about how you walk, can you suggest why the calf muscle is much larger than the shin muscle?

(h) If structure T was damaged or torn, how would this impair the movement of the foot?

148 The diagram below shows the skeleton of a breed of dog known as an Afghan hound.

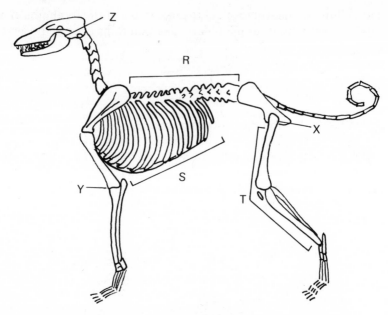

(a) What type of joint is found at points X, Y and Z on the skeleton?

(b) Give two functions of each of the parts labelled R, S and T.

(c) Afghan hounds are similar to greyhounds, but heavier in build and with a long coat. They hunt by sight, i.e. they watch their prey as it runs. Give one feature of the skeleton which shows their adaptation to this type of hunting.

149 Examine the diagram below showing a side view of part of the rib-cage of a human.

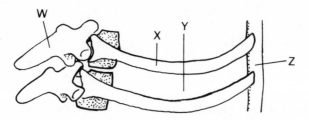

(a) What type of bone is W?

(b) What type of bone is X?

(c) What type of joint is found between W and X?

(d) Give one function for the bone labelled X?

(e) What is found in the space labelled Y?

(f) What is the function of these structures?

(g) What is Z?

EXTENSION QUESTION

150 The following diagrams show the skeletons of the forelimbs of a reptile, a bird and four mammals. The diagrams are not drawn to the same scale.

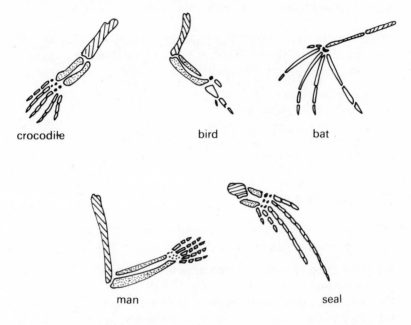

crocodile   bird   bat

man   seal

(a) Describe two features which you can see that are similar in the five skeletons.
(b) Name one feature in which the bat skeleton differs from that of man.
(c) What is the bat's forelimb specialised for?
(d) What other forelimb is similarly specialised?
(e) Give one difference between the bird's forelimb and the crocodile's.
(f) In Greek, 'penta' means five and 'dactilos' means finger. What does the term pentadactyl mean?
(g) Which of the limbs still retain all of the 'fingers'?

MULTIPLE CHOICE QUESTIONS

151 Which one of the following is **not** a hormone?

A adrenalin
B testosterone
C glycerol
D insulin
E progesterone

152 Which one of the following statements is **not** true of insulin?

    A   it is a hormone
    B   its absence causes diabetes
    C   it controls the sugar level in the blood
    D   it is only produced in adults
    E   it is produced in cells in the pancreas

153 Which one of the following changes in the body would **not** be brought about by the secretion into the blood of the hormone adrenalin from the adrenal glands?

    A   lower blood pressure
    B   higher blood sugar level
    C   dilation of blood capillaries of the heart
    D   constriction of blood capillaries of the skin
    E   dilation of the pupil

EXTENSION QUESTION

154 Which one of the following is **not** an example of homeostatic control in the human body?

    A   regulation of body temperature
    B   regulation of water level in the blood
    C   regulation of glucose level in the blood
    D   regulation of carbon dioxide in the blood
    E   regulation of body weight

STRUCTURED QUESTIONS

155 Diabetes mellitus is a condition in which the body is unable to metabolise sugars efficiently. It is caused by a deficiency of insulin. It is a disease which most commonly arises in people over forty years of age. The symptoms may be so slight that people are unaware that they have the disease.
Before insulin become available as injections, fewer than 20% of patients suffering severe diabetes lived more than ten years and children frequently lived less than a year. Symptoms of the disease include sugar in the urine and chemicals called ketones in the blood and urine.
Diabetics who delay their food intake or engage in heavy exercise can suffer from hypoglycaemia—a state where the sugar concentration in the blood decreases sharply.

    (a) What causes diabetes mellitus?
    (b) What age group of people are most likely to develop the disease?

(c) Does everyone who suffers from diabetes require medical treatment?
(d) What used to be the life expectancy for:
 (i) children who developed severe diabetes?
 (ii) adults who developed severe diabetes?
(e) How are these people kept alive today?
(f) Give two symptoms of diabetes.
(g) Why do diabetics sometimes need to be given sugar?

156 The diagram belows shows the assimilation of the main food classes in the body. It also indicates the effect of insulin on blood sugar and the effect of adrenalin.

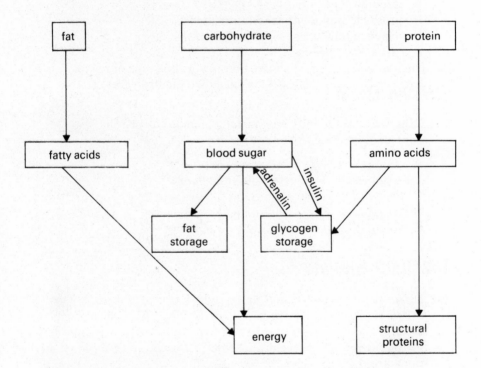

(a) Give two sources of energy shown in the diagram.
(b) What do insulin and adrenalin have in common?
(c) What effect does adrenalin have on blood sugar levels?
(d) In what kind of situation might it have this effect?
(e) Apart from that indicated on the diagram, give two ways in which insulin affects blood sugar.
(f) What would happen to the blood sugar level in the absence of insulin?
(g) What name is given to the disease suffered by people who cannot produce insulin?
(h) Give two ways in which this disease can be treated.

Theme 4
Development and Continuity of Life

MULTIPLE CHOICE QUESTIONS

1 In which one of the following is mitosis **not** involved?

A egg production in the ovary
B replacement of epidermis in the skin
C growth
D production of identical daughter cells
E tissue repair

2 The following diagram shows four stages in a type of nuclear division. (Two pairs of chromosomes are illustrated.)

 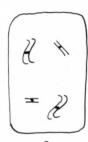  

| 1 | 2 | 3 | 4 |

Which of the following gives the correct order for the four stages?

A 2, 3, 4, 1
B 1, 2, 3, 4
C 4, 3, 2, 1
D 3, 4, 1, 2
E 4, 2, 1, 3

3 If an organism with a diploid number of chromosomes of 144 produced four cells by meiosis, how many chromosomes would each cell have?

A 144   B 72   C 288   D 216   E 36

4   Which of the following is **not** a characteristic of meiosis?

A   chromosomes arrange themselves in pairs
B   produces daughter cells with half the normal number of chromosomes
C   consists of two divisions, one after the other
D   occurs in cells throughout the body
E   allows the reassortment of characteristics in the offspring

5   Fruit fly eggs contain 4 chromosomes; dividing cells of onion root tips contain 16 chromosomes; crocus pollen grains have 3 chromosomes and hyacinth palisade cell nuclei have 16 chromosomes. Which one of the following correctly lists the diploid (2n) number of chromosomes in the organisms listed above in the corresponding order?

A   4, 8, 6, 16
B   8, 8, 6, 8
C   8, 16, 6, 16
D   8, 16, 6, 8
E   4, 8, 3, 8

EXTENSION QUESTION

6   In which one of the following regions of a plant would actively dividing cells **not** be found?

A   bud
B   shoot meristem
C   root meristem
D   cambium
E   stem pith

STRUCTURED QUESTIONS

7   Consider a single diploid cell that is about to perform cell division.

(a) If it performs *mitotic division*:
   (i) How many cells will be produced?
   (ii) What relative number of chromosomes will each new cell contain?
(b) If it performs *meiotic division*:
   (i) How many cells will be produced?
   (ii) What relative number of chromosomes will each new cell contain?

EXTENSION QUESTION

8 There are two types of cell division, known as *mitosis* and *meiosis*. They both produce an increase in the number of cells, but do so in a different way and for a different purpose.

(a) Consider the processes of cell division in a flowering plant.
- (i) Where would you expect to find mitosis occurring in the stem?
- (ii) Where would you expect to find mitosis occurring in the root?
- (iii) What purpose does cell division serve in these regions?
- (iv) In what two parts of the flower would you expect to find meiosis occurring?
- (v) What purpose does this meiotic cell division serve here?

(b) Consider the processes of cell division in a mammal.
- (i) In what parts of the body might you find the highest rates of mitosis?
- (ii) What function does mitosis perform in a mature mammal?
- (iii) What function does mitosis perform in a young mammal?
- (iv) Where does meiosis occur in male and female mammals?
- (v) What purpose does this meiotic cell division serve here?

MULTIPLE CHOICE QUESTIONS

9 Which of the following is usually true of cancer cells?

- A they are very large cells
- B they have no nucleus
- C they always occur in the lung
- D they cannot undergo mitosis
- E they have an increased growth rate

10 Which one of the following statements is **not** true about cancer?

- A it may be treated surgically or by chemotherapy
- B it is always fatal in the end
- C it may be caused by excessive sunlight (UV light)
- D it can be caused by chemicals in cigarette smoke
- E it can affect various parts of the body

11   Which one of the following is the best definition of a carcinogen?

   A   a substance which prevents cell division
   B   an inhibitor of mitosis
   C   an agent which causes cell division to get out of control
   D   a chemical causing damage to the germinal layer of the skin
   E   a substance which prevents cell wall formation

STRUCTURED QUESTIONS

12   Some time ago, shoe shops used to have X-ray machines.
      They were used to allow customers to see their toes inside new
      shoes when they were being tried on. The machines were banned
      from shoe shops when it was realised that they were potentially
      dangerous.

   (a) Why do you think the X-ray machines were potentially
       dangerous?
   (b) What kind of customer do you think may have been most at
       risk?
   (c) What kind of tissue was most likely to be damaged in such
       customers?
   (d) What do you call an agent or substance which causes the kind
       of damage that X-rays may induce?

EXTENSION QUESTION

13   Cancer is an abnormal growth in the body where some cells start
      to grow, multiply and spread. Cancerous cells sometimes grow into
      a lump, called a tumour.

   (a) Explain briefly what is meant by:
       (i) a malignant tumour
       (ii) a benign tumour.
   (b) What is a carcinogen? Explain briefly, giving two examples.
   (c) People who suffer from cancer are treated in two main ways.
       What is:
       (i) radiation therapy?
       (ii) chemotherapy?
   (d) Each of the forms of treatment has one or more disadvantages,
       as well as the obvious advantage. Give one disadvantage of:
       (i) radiation therapy
       (ii) chemotherapy.
   (e) What is 'screening'?

14 Which of the following is the best definition of sexual reproduction?

A the production of offspring by the fusion of two gametes
B the production of offspring from two parents
C the production of offspring from one parent
D the production of offspring by the fusion of two zygotes
E the production of offspring from two cells

15 The major difference between sexual reproduction and asexual reproduction is that:

A sexual reproduction involves pollination
B asexual reproduction is faster
C sexual reproduction occurs in animals
D asexual reproduction does not involve fertilisation
E sexual reproduction is more reliable

16 Which of the following is **not** a characteristic of wind-pollinated flowers?

A small flowers
B fine, light pollen
C bright colour
D large quantities of pollen
E anthers which hang outside the flower

17 Which one of the following is **not** involved in asexual reproduction?

A bulb   B corm   C rhizome   D runner   E seed

EXTENSION QUESTION

18 Which one of the following statements about reproduction in plants is correct?

A individual plants can only reproduce either sexually or asexually
B plants can reproduce asexually without producing flowers
C plants which reproduce sexually must have some means of attracting insects
D all the ovules produced by an individual flower must be fertilised in order for any of them to develop
E all plants produce seeds every year

19 Examine the following diagram which shows a longitudinal section through a single flower from the head of a dandelion.

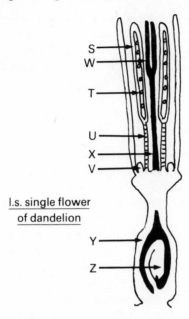

l.s. single flower
of dandelion

(a) Name the structures S–Z.
(b) Which letters refer to the 'male' parts of the flower?
(c) Which letters refer to the 'female' parts of the flower?
(d) Which part becomes the seed?
(e) Give one feature which suggests that this flower is insect-pollinated.

20 A flower is the organ of sexual reproduction in a flowering plant. Name the following parts of an insect-pollinated flower from the descriptions provided.

(a) Large, coloured part.
(b) The parts which make the pollen.
(c) The sweet, sticky liquid in some flowers.
(d) The part on which the pollen sticks.
(e) The part which contains the female sex cells.
(f) The little stalk which supports the part which makes the pollen.
(g) The little 'leaves' around the flower which are often green.
(h) The part through which the pollen tubes must grow to reach the female sex cells.
(i) The name of the female sex cell.
(j) The name of the part which makes the pollen, together with its stalk.

21 Creeping buttercup is a common weed of pastures and lawns. The diagram below shows the shoots and root system of a single buttercup plant and its daughters.

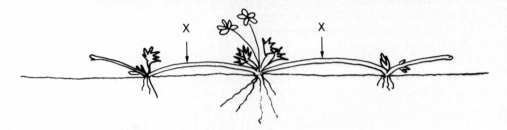

(a) Name the structures labelled X.

(b) What name is given to the type of reproduction shown by creeping buttercup?

(c) Explain carefully how the structures labelled X are involved in this reproduction.

(d) Give one reason why creeping buttercup is able to spread over a field quickly.

(e) Give one reason why the presence of creeping buttercup makes it difficult for other plants to grow.

(f) Creeping buttercup also produces flowers.
   (i) What type of reproduction requires flowers?
   (ii) What is the connection between flower production and creeping buttercup's ability to colonise new fields?

Examine the following diagram of a section through a flower.

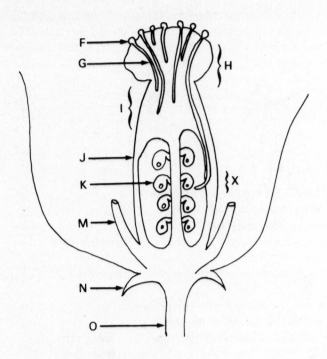

(a) Name the structures labelled F–O.
(b) What collective name can be used to describe structures H, I and J?
(c) What is the name given to the process by which structure F came to be on structure H?
(d) What process is about to occur in the region labelled X?
(e) Explain briefly what will happen.
(f) A few weeks later, the structures shown in the diagram will have changed into a pea pod.
Assuming that *all* relevant structures are shown in the diagram,
  (i) how many peas will there be in the pod when it is opened?
  (ii) Explain how you arrived at this number.
  (iii) Which structures shown in the diagram have become peas?
  (iv) Which structure do you think has become the pod?
  (v) Pea pods do not always contain the same number of peas. Suggest two reasons for this.

EXTENSION QUESTION

23 The following drawings are of five different named flowers. The questions which follow can be answered by careful inspection of these diagrams. Note that the word 'receptacle' refers to the end of the flower stalk, which may have different shapes in different species.

FLOWER TYPES

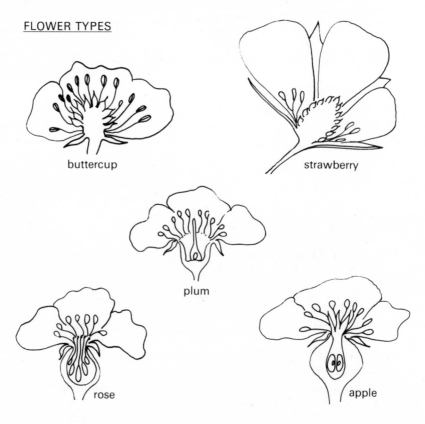

buttercup

strawberry

plum

rose

apple

(a) In which flower (or flowers) does the receptacle seem to have the ovary or ovaries on its surface?

(b) In which flower is there a single, undivided ovary?

(c) In which flower (or flowers) is there an ovary obviously divided into compartments?

(d) In which flower (or flowers) are there many ovaries?

(e) Assuming that the drawings are all to the same scale, give four differences between a strawberry flower and a buttercup flower.

(f) There follows diagrams of five fruits produced from the flowers shown above. Examine each fruit carefully and match the letters to the names of the flowers to indicate which flower produces which fruit.

FRUIT TYPES

 P

 Q

 R

 S

 T

MULTIPLE CHOICE QUESTIONS

24 Which one of the following is **not** part of normal sexual reproduction or development in humans?

   A   the release of sperm inside the body of a woman
   B   the formation of an egg with a large yolk supply
   C   the fusion of a sperm and an egg in the oviduct
   D   the development of a placenta
   E   the implantation of a fertilised egg in the uterus

25 Which one of the following pairs correctly shows a reproductive structure and its function?

   A   uterus—embryo development
   B   testis—egg production
   C   ureter—sperm production
   D   oviduct—implantation
   E   vagina—fertilisation

26 Which one of the following is **not** an example of a sexually-transmitted disease?

   A   gonorrhea
   B   AIDS
   C   genital herpes
   D   syphilis
   E   tuberculosis

27 Which one of the following contraceptive methods relies for its effect on stopping sperm travelling from the testes to the urethra?

    A   hysterectomy
    B   intra-uterine device
    C   vasectomy
    D   condom
    E   oral contraceptive pill

EXTENSION QUESTION

28 A woman gives birth to sextuplets consisting of three girls and three boys. Which one of the following descriptions of the genetic relationship between the children is correct?

    A   they are genetically identical
    B   they are clones
    C   they are cousins
    D   they are brothers and sisters
    E   they are half-brothers and half-sisters

STRUCTURED QUESTIONS

29 Sperm and eggs are specialised cells, called sex cells or gametes. The following table lists some characteristics which may apply to both sperm and eggs or only to one. Copy out the table and place a tick in the column you think most appropriate. One tick has been added for you.

Characteristic	Applies to		
	Egg	Sperm	Both
Has a cell membrane			✓
Has a tail			
Will die if no fertilisation occurs			
Usually has a large store of food			
Produced by females			
Can swim			
Produced by males			

30 Copy out the following table and fill it in using the terms given below. Some terms may be used more than once. Give an example of each type of animal in the first column.

Type of animal	Example	Number of eggs	Size of egg	Food supply for embryo	Oxygen supply for embryo
Mammal					
Fish					
Bird					
Amphibian					

Relative number of eggs: very numerous, numerous, few
Relative size of egg: large, medium, small, microscopic
Food supply: outside the egg, inside the egg, from the mother
Oxygen supply: outside the egg, inside the egg, from the mother

31 The diagram below shows the human male reproductive system.

(a) Name the structures U–Y.
(b) Which part is responsible for the manufacture of sperm?
(c) Which part is responsible for the transport of sperm?
(d) Which part is responsible for manufacturing the fluid in which the sperm swim?
(e) Which part is responsible for transferring the sperm into the female during copulation (sexual intercourse)?
(f) What change must happen to this structure before it can be used for sexual intercourse?
(g) Into which structure of the female reproductive system would sperm be deposited (ejaculated) during sexual intercourse?
(h) Give two kinds of contraception, one permanent and one temporary, which may be used by males.

32 The diagram below shows the reproductive system of a female human (1) and a female rat (2).

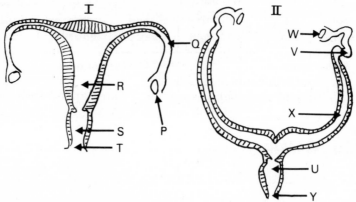

(a) Name the structures P–Y.
(b) Give one letter from each diagram to show where eggs (ova) are produced.
(c) Give one letter from each diagram to show where embryos may develop.
(d) Give one letter from each diagram to show where male and female sex cells (gametes) meet.
(e) Give two differences between the human and the rat female reproductive systems, as shown in the diagram.
(f) Where are sperm released into the human female reproductive system?
(g) Give two methods of contraception, one permanent and one temporary, which may be used by women to avoid pregnancy.

MULTIPLE CHOICE QUESTIONS

33 Which one of the following sets of conditions is essential for seed germination?

    A   oxygen, water, light
    B   supply of water, adequate light, carbon dioxide
    C   sunlight, warmth, carbon dioxide
    D   sunlight, warmth, oxygen
    E   supply of water, suitable temperature, oxygen

34 In seeds, food may be stored in the:

    A   radicle   D   plumule
    B   cotyledon   E   micropyle
    C   testa

35 In the germination of a seed, which one of the following gives the correct order of events?

A   appearance of radicle, splitting of seed coat, absorption of water, appearance of plumule

B   absorption of water, splitting of seed coat, appearance of radicle, appearance of plumule

C   splitting of seed coat, appearance of radicle, absorption of water, appearance of plumule

D   absorption of water, splitting of seed coat, appearance of plumule, appearance of radicle

E   splitting of seed coat, absorption of water, appearance of radicle, appearance of plumule

EXTENSION QUESTION

36 When a seed first breaks its dormancy it:

A   increases its dry weight

B   decreases its fresh weight

C   begins to respire

D   decreases its dry weight

E   begins to photosynthesise

STRUCTURED QUESTIONS

37 A group of forty dried broad-bean seeds were selected from hundreds to be used in an experiment. They were picked because they were all of a similar size and looked healthy. They were divided into two equal-sized batches, M and N. Batch M were untouched but batch N seeds all had their seed coats (or testa) carefully removed. All seeds were then placed in a warm, moist, dark place for five days. When they were examined, the numbers of seeds that had germinated were counted. The results are summarised in the following table.

	Germinated	Non-germinated
Batch M	12	8
Batch N	20	0

Now answer the following questions.

(a) What percentage of batch M seeds germinated? Show your calculation.

(b) What percentage of batch N seeds germinated? Show your calculation.

(c) Explain why more batch N seeds than batch M seeds germinated.

(d) What do you think is the usual function of the seed coat with respect to seed germination?

(e) What hypothesis do you think this experiment was designed to test?

38 Examine the following diagrams of fruits.

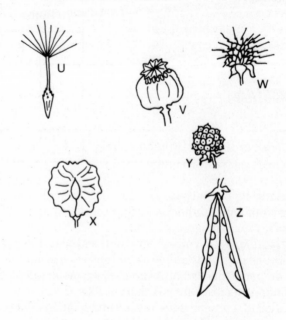

Copy out the table and fill in the blanks, using the information contained in the diagrams.

Fruit	Dispersal method	Special adaptation
U		
		Seed coat extended (wing)
	Self	
		Seeds in capsule
	Animal	
W		

39 In an experiment, two identical petri dishes were set up and labelled A and B. Filter paper was placed in the base of each dish, distilled water poured in to soak the paper, and then excess water drained off. Ten barley seeds were placed in dish A and one hundred in dish B. The lids were replaced and both dishes were kept in a dark cupboard for one week.
The results were as follows.

	Dish	
	A	B
Number germinated	6	43
Maximum length of roots/mm	30	10
Maximum length of shoots/mm	45	0

(a) Calculate the percentage germination for each dish.
(b) Apart from water, what two other requirements are *always* necessary for seed germination?
(c) Explain as fully as you can any noticeable difference in the percentage germination between the two dishes.
(d) Why do you think the roots and shoots were longer in the germinated seeds of dish A than in dish B?
(e) Several of the ungerminated seeds in dish B had a blue mould growing on them. Why do you think this occurred in dish B but not in dish A?

40 Some seeds are commonly found on beaches. One group of such seeds, sometimes called 'sea-beans', are to be found on the beaches of the west of Ireland and the Outer Hebrides. These sea-beans are the seeds of tropical vines found growing in the Caribbean. They have a very thick seed coat, or testa, and always have an air-filled cavity inside the testa.

(a) Describe how these seeds are dispersed.
(b) What is the function of the inner air-filled cavity?
(c) What is the function of the thick seed coat?
(d) How, when they live and grow in the Caribbean, do they find their way to the British Isles?
(e) Name three environmental conditions that it is necessary to provide to allow a seed, such as the sea-bean, to germinate.
(f) Why do sea-beans not normally germinate when washed up on Irish beaches?

41 A holly seedling, like the one shown in the diagram below, was found growing beneath a hedge.

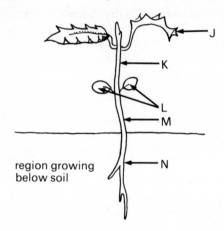

(a) Name the parts labelled J–N.

(b) What type of germination is shown by this seedling? Explain your answer.

(c) What do the structures labelled J and L have in common?

(d) What group of flowering plants does this seedling belong to? What characteristic of the seedling allows this identification?

(e) Explain how the seedling may have come to grow beneath the hedge in which there were no other holly trees.

42 Copy out the diagram below and place the following terms in the appropriate boxes.

A seed germination
B fruit and seed dispersal
C fertilization
D pollination

E flower formation
F pollen tube growth
G fruit and seed formation
H plant growth

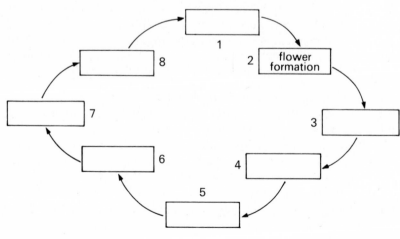

EXTENSION QUESTION

43 The diagram below refers to a deciduous woodland. The letters indicate the months of the year, starting with J for January. The numbers represent different species of plant growing in this woodland.

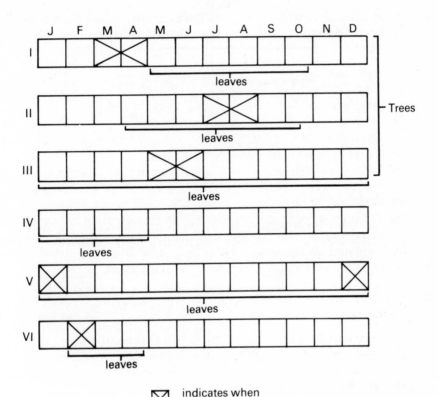

indicates when flowers are present

(a) Which of the numbers indicate deciduous trees?

(b) Which of the trees is most likely to be wind-pollinated?

(c) Explain your answer to **(b)**.

(d) Which of the numbers indicate a plant other than a flowering plant?

(e) Explain your answer to **(d)**.

(f) Which of the numbers indicate a plant such as a snowdrop or crocus?

(g) Give one reason for your answer to **(f)**.

(h) Which of the plants is most likely to be the one known as the Christmas rose?

149

44 Which of the following organisms' young are cared for by the parents?

    A lion   B cuckoo   C herring   D turtle   E frog

45 After a human baby is born, another structure called the afterbirth must be delivered from the mother. The afterbirth can also be called the:

    A amniotic sac
    B umbilical cord
    C amniotic fluid
    D uterus
    E placenta

46 Which one of the following is **not** a function of the mammalian placenta?

    A prevents the mixing of the mother's and the embryo's blood
    B prevents entry of bacteria into the developing embryo
    C supplies oxygen to the developing embryo
    D respires and releases energy for the developing embryo
    E takes away the waste products of the developing embryo

EXTENSION QUESTION

47 Which one of the following combinations bests describes what happens to a human embryo during the last month of its development?

	Cells	Tissues	Organs
A	become smaller	become larger	become larger
B	become smaller	become larger	become more numerous
C	become fewer	become more numerous	become larger
D	become more numerous	become fewer	become more numerous
E	become more numerous	become larger	become larger

48 The following diagrams show stages in the development of a chick.

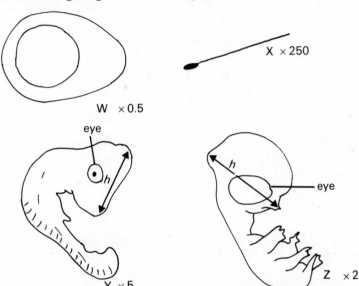

W ×0.5

X × 250

eye

Y ×5

Z ×2

(a) Using a ruler and the magnification figures given on the diagrams, copy out and complete the table below. (Note: Measure the head sizes along the line labelled h on the diagrams; measure the eyes at the widest points.)

Diagram	Name	Length on diagram/mm	Actual size /mm
	Egg		
	Sperm		
	Head of $3\frac{1}{2}$ day-old chick		
	Eye of $3\frac{1}{2}$ day-old chick		
	Head of 7 day-old chick		
	Eye of 7 day-old chick		

(b) Approximately how many times larger is the egg compared to the sperm?

(c) How does the size of the eye in the 7 day-old chick compare with that in the $3\frac{1}{2}$ day-old chick?

49 The diagram below shows a mammalian embryo.

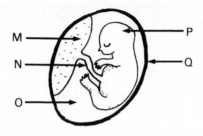

(a) Name the structures indicated on the diagram.
(b) Give two functions for the structure labelled M.
(c) Give one function for:
  (i) N
  (ii) O
  (iii) Q.
(d) Give one reason why the embryo is not in direct contact with its mother's blood system.

50 (a) What is the definition of gestation time (pregnancy) for animals?
(b) What sort of animals have a gestation time?
(c) Look at this table, which shows the gestation time for various animals.

Animal	Mouse	Dog	Pig	Human	Horse	Blue whale	Elephant
Gestation time/weeks	3	8	18	36	48	80	96

  (i) What is the general relationship between body size and gestation time?
  (ii) What animal in the table is an exception to this general rule?

EXTENSION QUESTION

51 (a) The following table shows the average weight of boys and girls from birth to two years old.

152

Age/months		0	4	8	12	16	20	24
Weight/ kg	Boys	3.6	6.6	8.8	10.2	11.2	11.9	12.6
	Girls	3.4	6.0	8.2	9.6	10.6	11.5	12.1

   (i) Plot these results on a graph and join up the points to show a comparison of the weights for boys and girls.

  (ii) At what age is the difference in body weight between boys and girls least?

 (iii) Is it possible that a ten month old girl could be heavier than a ten month old boy? Explain your answer.

(b) The following table shows the average weight of boys and girls from 8 to 16 years.

Age/years		8	9	10	11	12	13	14	15	16
Weight/ kg	Boys	27.4	29.9	32.6	35.2	38.3	42.2	48.8	54.5	58.8
	Girls	26.4	28.9	31.9	35.7	39.7	45.0	49.2	51.5	53.1

   (i) As far as weight is concerned, when do girls start to catch up with boys?

  (ii) When do they weigh more than boys?

 (iii) How do you account for girls being heavier than boys during this time?

 (iv) What other changes, apart from size, are likely to be taking place for girls about this age?

MULTIPLE CHOICE QUESTIONS

52 Male mammals result from the inheritance of:

  A an X chromosome from the father and a Y chromosome from the mother

  B an X chromosome from the father and an X chromosome from the mother

  C a Y chromosome from the father and a Y chromosome from the mother

  D a Y chromosome from the father and an X chromosome from the mother

  E a Y chromosome from the father and no chromosome from the mother

53 Which one of the following human variations **cannot** be inherited?

A blood group
B left-handedness
C length of hair
D intelligence
E sex

54 The term *genotype* is best defined as:

A the alleles carried by an organism
B the chromosomes carried by an organism
C the inherited appearance of an organism
D a heterozygous organism
E the dominant genes of an organism

55 A dominant gene is one which:

A dominates behaviour
B influences the phenotype
C is only found in a homozygous condition
D always partners a recessive gene
E is only found in a heterozygous condition

EXTENSION QUESTION

56 Colour blindness is a sex-linked condition caused by a recessive allele. Which one of the following correctly gives the percentage probability of a colour blind man and his wife who has normal vision having a son who is colour blind?

A 25%   B 50%   C 75%   D 100%   E 0%

STRUCTURED QUESTIONS

57 Gregor Mendel was the first person to demonstrate the laws of inheritance. He did this by carrying out a large number of breeding experiments on pea plants. One of the characteristics he investigated was the height of the plant stems.
When he cross-pollinated pure-breeding tall plants with pure-breeding short plants, he found they gave rise to a generation of tall plants only. When he later self-pollinated this generation, he found the second generation produced contained tall and short plants in the ratio 3:1.

(a) Which characteristic for height was dominant?
(b) What alternative term can be used for 'pure-breeding'?

(c) What was the genotype of the first generation of tall plants produced?

(d) What genotypes were present in the second generation produced?

(e) What do you call alternative forms of the same gene for a characteristic such as height?

58 Seeds of garden peas may be either round or wrinkled, as illustrated below.

In an attempt to find out more about the genetics of garden peas, a gardener selected one pod for further investigation. The pod selected contained 8 round seeds, which were planted the following spring. At flowering time, the gardener allowed the plants to self-pollinate, and at harvest time he collected all the pods and examined their contents. In all, 76 pods were harvested. The table below shows the contents of 8 pods selected at random.

Code letter of pod		S	T	U	V	W	X	Y	Z
Contents of each pod	Round	7	4	8	5	3	4	5	6
	Wrinkled	1	4	0	2	3	2	1	1

Now answer these questions.

(a) What is meant by the term 'self-pollinate'?

(b) Describe how the gardener ensured that this occurred.

(c) What is the total number of round peas?

(d) What is the total number of wrinkled peas?

(e) What is the average number of peas per pod?

(f) What is the ratio of round peas to wrinkled peas?

(g) Explain how this ratio occurred—use a diagram to illustrate your answer.

(h) Describe clearly what further steps the gardener could take to determine the genotype of the seeds in pod U.

59 Common domestic cats may be long haired or short haired. It is assumed that these characteristics are inherited in a normal Mendelian fashion by a single pair of alleles. A long haired tom cat (male) was crossed with a short haired queen (female) and all the offspring were found to be short haired.

In your answers to the following questions, you may use the symbol S for the dominant allele and s for the recessive allele.

(a) Which is the dominant characteristic, and how do you know?

(b) Predict the genotype of the short haired offspring of the cross.

(c) Explain what could be done practically to establish the genotype of these short haired cats and what results would be expected.

(d) What ratio of phenotypes would be expected if two of these short haired types were crossed?

60 In Afghan hounds (a breed of dog), the basic coat colour can be overlaid with a striped pattern, known as brindle. Brindling (B) is dominant to the non-brindle condition (b). The following is part of the pedigree of two Afghan hounds.

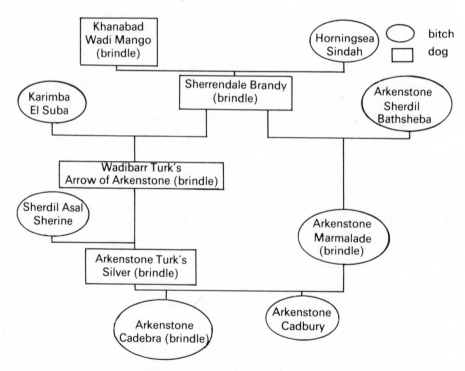

(a) What is the relationship between Arkenstone Cadebra and Arkenstone Cadbury?

(b) What is the relationship between Wadibarr Turk's Arrow of Arkenstone and Arkenstone Marmalade?

(c) What is the genotype of Arkenstone Cadbury and Sherdil Asal Sherine?

(d) What is the genotype of Arkenstone Turk's Silver?

(e) Give two reasons why you know that Arkenstone Marmalade must have been heterozygous.

61 In Afghan hounds, black coat colour is dominant over a colour combination known as black and tan. In a litter of pups, six were black and four were black and tan. The father of these pups was a black dog.

(a) Is the father homozygous or heterozygous?

(b) Explain your answer to (a).

(c) If the mother is homozygous, what is her genotype?

(d) What would be the genotype of all the black pups?

(e) What would be the genotype of all the black and tan pups?

(f) Show diagrammatically what you would expect to get if one of the black pups was crossed with one of the black and tan pups.

62 The ABO blood groups fall into four different phenotypes: A, B, AB and O. The two alleles A and B are equally dominant, but O is recessive to both A and B. Every person must carry any two of these three alleles.

(a) What blood groups might children inherit from parents who are group AB and O?

(b) What genotypes might these children have?

(c) What two genotypes might produce blood group A?

(d) What two genotypes might produce blood group B?

(e) What are the chances of a person with blood group A being homozygous for this characteristic?

63 Haemophilia is a disease which slows blood clotting time. The normal gene for blood clotting is carried on the X-chromosome but not on the Y-chromosome. The gene for haemophilia (n) is recessive to the gene for normal blood clotting (N). Females have two X chromosomes, while males have one X and one Y chromosome.

(a) Give the genotype of a male with the normal ability to clot blood.

(b) Give the genotype of a haemophiliac male.

(c) Give the two possible genotypes for females who are able to clot blood normally.

(d) What term can be used for a female who is able to produce haemophiliac sons?

(e) What term can be used for inheritance that is related to X and Y chromosomes?

64 Horses do not normally carry a gene for striped coats.
In 1821, Lord Marston reported to the Royal Society the results of
mating a quagga (a species of zebra, now extinct) to a brown mare.
The result of the mating was a foal with stripes. He reported that
the same mare was later mated to a black stallion and two foals
were produced which were also striped. Professor Ewart, in 1899,
repeated the experiment (ten times) but found that, while the
zebra–mare cross always produced a striped foal, there were
never any stripes in the offspring when the mare was mated with a
black stallion.

(a) How do you explain the first striped foal produced by Lord
Marston?

(b) Why was the result of Lord Marston's second breeding
experiment unexpected?

(c) Why did Professor Ewart find no evidence of striping in the
second part of his breeding experiment (black stallion/mare)?

(d) Using the letter S for striping and s for no striping, show by
means of a diagram the result of Lord Marston's first breeding
experiment quagga/mare), assuming the quagga was
homozygous.

(e) Show by means of a diagram the results obtained by Professor
Ewart in his breeding experiment (black stallion/mare).

(f) Why did Professor Ewart repeat his experiment ten times?

(g) What genetic explanation may account for the result of Lord
Marston's second breeding experiment?

MULTIPLE CHOICE QUESTIONS

65 Which one of the following is **not** the result of selection by man?

    A   high milk yields in dairy cows
    B   high beef production in cattle
    C   high egg production by hens
    D   high egg production by marine fish
    E   high yielding cereal crops

66 Which one of the following is **not** the result of natural selection?

    A   plumage in wild birds
    B   nectaries in insect-pollinated flowers
    C   the size of elephants
    D   camouflage in butterflies
    E   modern varieties of apples

67 Cave-dwelling animals are often coloured white even though closely related species that do not live in caves are colourful and camouflaged. This can be explained by the action of:

A   artificial selection
B   artificial insemination
C   natural selection
D   increased mutation
E   aerobic respiration

68 A mutagen may best be defined as:

A   a chemical which influences inheritance
B   something which stimulates an inheritable change in genetic structure
C   a gene which undergoes a spontaneous change during meiosis
D   a random event which alters the pattern of inheritance
E   radiation which alters the pattern of inheritance

69 Genetic engineering involves:

A   adding a useful gene into the gene system of a harmless microbe for replication
B   constructing new chromosomes to form new animals
C   hybridisation of different animal or plant species
D   making new genes from the genetic code
E   test-tube (in vitro) fertilisation

EXTENSION QUESTION

70 Darwin's theory of evolution is based on three observations and two deductions, numbered 1–5 below.

1   Individuals in populations have a great reproductive potential.
2   Individuals in populations tend to remain relatively constant in number.
3   There is a struggle for existence in which many individuals in a population fail to reproduce.
4   Individuals with variations best adapted to their environment have a reproductive advantage.
5   Variations exist between individuals in populations.

Identify those statements which are observations and those which are deductions from the alternative answers given below.

	observations	deductions
A	1, 2, 3	4, 5
B	1, 2, 5	3, 4
C	2, 3, 4	1, 5
D	3, 4, 5	1, 2
E	2, 3, 5	1, 4

71 During the industrial revolution, air pollution altered the environment dramatically. Light forms of moths, which were previously widespread, became rare in industrial areas while dark forms became more abundant. This trend has been reversed since the introduction of the Clean Air Act of 1965. It is known that both light and dark forms of moths are preyed upon by birds.

(a) What acted as a selective agent in bringing about the decline in the number of light forms of moths?

(b) What advantage did the light forms have before they started to become rare in industrial locations?

(c) In what sort of area would the light forms have retained this advantage?

(d) Why did the dark forms become more abundant in industrial areas?

(e) Why has this trend in the abundance of light and dark forms of moths been reversed since 1965?

72 The following descriptions of tomato varieties come from a seed catalogue.

Variety	Flavour	Food value	Crop size	Tomato size	Disease resistance
Ailsa Craig	Medium	High	Heavy	Average	Low
Supercross	Medium	Medium	Very heavy	Average	High
Small Fry	Very good	Very high	Heavy	Very small	Low
Gardener's Delight	Supreme	Maximum	Heavy	Average	Low
Spring Giant	Very good	Medium	Very heavy	Very large	High

(a) Which variety has the best food value?

(b) Give one disadvantage of this variety.

(c) Assuming all varieties can be cross-pollinated, which two varieties would you cross to produce plants which have the characteristics of high disease resistance, the best flavour and the largest tomatoes?

(d) What two varieties might give you the worst combination of characteristics for disease resistance, tomato size and flavour?

(e) What term can be used for choosing the parent characteristics to produce a new and improved variety?

73 The Bible tells a story of how Jacob attempted to produce spotted cattle. He tried to influence pregnant cattle in a herd by placing stakes about their pen which had white markings on them. The result, we are told, was that many spotted offspring were born from whole-coloured mothers.

(a) Why would stock breeders today not use this method for influencing the colour of offspring?
(b) What term could be used to describe the spotted characteristic of offspring if both parents were whole-coloured?
(c) What term would be used to describe such parents?
(d) Assuming that the spotted characteristic was caused by a single gene, what proportion of offspring would be spotted if they were produced from two whole-coloured parents?
(e) What is the most likely explanation of the large number of spotted offspring produced by Jacob's cattle?

EXTENSION QUESTION

74

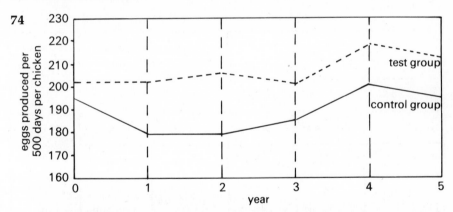

The figure above shows the results of a poultry breeding experiment. From an initial large population of poultry, two groups were chosen. The control group were chosen completely at random; the test group consisted of those chickens which had laid most eggs in the previous year.

In each subsequent year, the control group were allowed to breed at random, but only the most efficient layers in the test group were allowed to mate. The offspring of year 0 became the experimental chickens in year 1, and so on. This regime continued for six years, as shown above.

(a) Why is the number of eggs produced per chicken lower in the control group than in the test group in year 0?

(b) Why were the control group allowed to mate at random?

(c) Can you suggest why only the best egg layers of the test group were allowed to breed?

(d) What is the difference between number of eggs laid by the test group in year 5, compared to year 0?

(e) Why was it necessary to have a control group in this experiment?

(f) What term is used to describe this type of breeding experiment?

ANSWERS

Theme 1
Diversity

1	D	**2**	C	**3**	B	**4**	A
5	C	**6**	D	**7**	E	**8**	C
9	A						

10 (a) M mollusc; R annelid;
S flatworm; T spider; U insect;
V coelenterate; X starfish;
Y crustacean

(b) W

(c) It is a vertebrate/amphibian.

11 M Albertosaurus; R Scelidosaurus;
S Psittacosaurus;
T Stenonchosaurus;
U Apatosaurus;
V Triceratops; W Euoplocephalus

12 I mayfly nymph; II great diving
beetle larva; III whirligig beetle
larva; IV stone fly nymph; V damsel
fly nymph; VI alder fly nymph

13 M sycamore; R alder; S willow;
T oak; U lilac; V sweet chestnut

14 (a) M scarlet fly cap; R milk white
russula; S sickener; T fleecy
milk cap; U parrot wax cap;
V scarlet wax cap

(b) Colour of spores

(c) They all have white spores.

(d) Sickener is poisonous; scarlet
wax cap is not.

15 See Table A1 below

16 (a) Molluscs (b) Muscular foot
and shell (c) Shell

(d) Internal shell in T

17 (a) (i) M (ii) T and S (iii) R

(b) (i) None (ii) M (iii) R (iv) T and S

(c) M, S and T

(d) M (e) S

(f) Spider's body divided into two
parts, insect's body divided into
three parts; spiders have four
pairs of legs, insects have three
pairs of legs

(g) Jointed legs; hard outside
skeleton

(h) (i) R (ii) S (iii) M (iv) T

18 (a) R (b) V (c) T and U

(d) Y and Z (e) R, T, U and W

(f) X and Y (g) S, X, Y and Z

(h) W (i) S and W (j) U

19 (a) M antenna/feeler; R eye;
S thorax; T wing; W abdomen

(b) (i) Investigate the surroundings/
smell/touch (ii) See

(c) To protect the delicate flying
wings when the insect is
crawling through the leaf litter

(d) Wings; body divided into three
parts

20 (a) Internal bony skeleton; dorsal
hollow nerve cord (or any other
acceptable vertebrate or
chordate structure)

(b) Use their hard beak or bill

(c) Mammals

(d) Fish, amphibians and reptiles

(e) Bat

(f) (i) Flight (ii) Heat insulation

21 (a) Gills/scales/fins

(b) Cold-blooded

mammals	B	body covered with fur
fungi	I	no chlorophyll; spores
algae	M	no stems or roots; many colours
molluscs	F	shell
flowering plants	J	plants with flowers
birds	K	feathers; wings
reptiles	L	scaly skin
ferns	A	roots; spores
amphibians	G	thin skin; lay eggs in water
fish	H	scales; fins
mosses	E	no stems or roots
true worms	C	body segmented; no legs
conifers	D	bear cones

Table A1

(c) (i) Front fins (ii) Swim bladder
(iii) Stopping and swimming
backwards
(iv) Cannot see in colour
(v) Plenty of food
(vi) To identify members of the
same species

22 (a) Plants are autotrophic and can
synthesise their own food;
animals are heterotrophic and
must ingest organic material.

(b) Plant cell has cell wall, animal
cell has not; plant cell has inner
cell membrane surrounding a
sap-filled vacuole, animal cell
has not; plant cells contain
chloroplasts in their cytoplasm,
animal cells do not; plant cells
may have a more regular shape
than animal cells.

(c) (i) Algae
(ii) Any moss or liverwort, e.g.
wall moss.
(iii) Any fern (horsetail or
clubmoss), e.g. tongue fern.
(iv) They have vascular tissue
which can supply nutrients up
a long stem and give support.
(v) Spermatophytes
(flowering plants)

23 A chaetae (bristles);
B central digestive system;
C muscle; D dorsal blood vessel;
E muscle; F ventral blood vessel;
G ventral nerve cord

24 (a) A   (b) B   (c) C   (d) C
(e) A   (f) B   (g) C   (h) C
(i) A   (j) C   (k) A

Theme 2
Inter-relationships

1 D   2 E   3 C   4 B
5 (a)

owl	owl	owl	t. consumer
↑	↑	↑	↑
thrush	thrush	thrush	s. consumer
↑	↑	↑	↑
caterpillars	caterpillars	snails	p. consumer
↑	↑	↑	↑
dandelion	clover	clover	producer

(b) (i) Dandelion, clover or grass,
depending on answer to (a)
(ii) Mice, voles, snails or
caterpillars, depending on
answer to (a)
(iii) Stoat or owl

(c) grass→snails

6 (a) Microscopic plants→
protozoa→mosquito larvae→
coelenterates→water
boatmen→perch

(b) Mayfly nymphs, protozoa

(c) Mosquito larvae, tadpoles

(d) Mosquito larvae, tadpoles

(e) Small fish, water beetles, great
diving beetle, perch, water
boatmen, coelenterates

(f) 3 (protozoa, arthropods,
coelenterates)

(g) 2 (fish, amphibians)

7 (a) diatom→water flea→
water mite→mayfly nymph→
water boatman

(b)
area	animals
surface	1
pond water	7, 4
mud	3, 5
gravel	8
weeds	6, 2

8 (a) Oak trees, heather, brambles,
nettles

(b) Slugs, mice, bees

(c) Heather→slugs→hedgehogs
Brambles→mice→foxes
(or other suitable example)

(d) Fungi

(e) Breakdown of complex organic
materials for re-use

(f) Use the dung as food; recycling

9 (a) (i) $x = 10\%$ (ii) $y = 10\%$

(b) 40%

(c) Herbivore's diet is made up
largely of cellulose, which is
poor quality food.

(d) 100 kg

(e) 50 kg

10 **(a)**

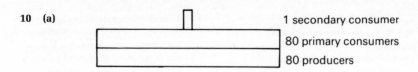

1 secondary consumer
80 primary consumers
80 producers

(b)

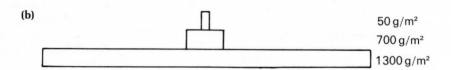

50 g/m²
700 g/m²
1300 g/m²

(c) Total biomass of a trophic level is not influenced by the size of individuals.

(d) Dry weight is preferable because wet weight is influenced by the water content of the individual.

(e) Heat in oven at less than 100 °C, weigh and reheat and reweigh until a constant mass is reached.

11 **(a)** B   **(b)** A   **(c)** C   **(d)** B
     (e) C   **(f)** C   **(g)** B   **(h)** A

12 B   **13** D   **14** C   **15** E

16 **(a)** W, T   **(b)** S, R   **(c)** Feeding
     (d) Absorption   **(e)** Decay
     (f) Denitrification

17 **(a)** Pasture
     (b) Bales of hay/grain
     (c) Cattle, hens
     (d) Manure heap
     (e) Fertiliser, manure heap
     (f) Hens, cattle
     (g) Farm dog, farmer
     (h) Respiration
     (i) Sunlight

18 **(a)** M photosynthesis;
       R respiration;
       S respiration;
       X combustion;
       Z respiration

     (b) Death, defaecation, excretion

     (c) Absence of oxygen

     (d) Decomposition. Fungi and bacteria

     (e) Lightning. Burning garden rubbish

     (f) M occurs at a much greater rate than R.

19 See diagram below.

20 **(a)** Nitrates, phosphates

     (b) Needed by plants for growth

     (c) Not sufficient photosynthesis/ too cold/not enough strong sunlight

     (d) Removal of bacteria

     (e) Primary consumer

21 A

22 E

Answer to question 19.

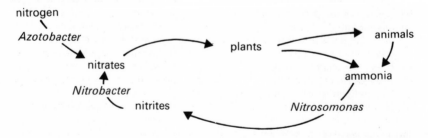

23 **(a)** C
(b) Adequate water/good humus content
(c) Air contains oxygen—necessary for root respiration and growth
(d) A
(e) Very permeable to water/low water and humus content
(f) For water retention and to provide minerals by decay

24 **(a)** (i) Air (ii) From the atmosphere (iii) So that only the difference in air flow in the soil samples is measured
(iv) Between stopper and flask; between tubes and stopper; at the outlet to the vacuum pump
(b) (i) Permeability to air/porosity
(ii) If it is not fresh, it may have dried out, therefore changing its permeability. Different soils dry out at different rates.
(iii) So that the comparison is valid
(iv) X: clay soil; Y: sandy soil

25 **(a)** Erosion by wind and rain
(b) High rainfall/steep slopes
(c) There is less soil in which to plant seed and grow crops. Plants will be less stable. Fewer minerals means poorer growth
(d) Plant trees again; terrace land

26 A **27** B **28** E

29 **(a)** 150 **(b)** 30
(c) No. worms in = 54 + 28
quadrats 2 and 3 = 82

No. worms = 82 ÷ 2
per m² = 41

So total   No. worms   Area of
no. worms = per m² × meadow
= 41 × 400
= 16 400 worms
(d) Ground trampled around sample 3, therefore more compacted and less worms
(e) Stony ground in quarry; disturbance by man in housing estate
(f) Not all the worms may have come up in each quadrat.

30 **(a)** Deborah could hear a lot of grasshoppers. Jonathan couldn't see any.
(b) The grasshoppers were hiding in the grass (Louise).

Grasshoppers like the shade (David).
(c) To compare the numbers in sunlight with numbers in shade (i.e. the sunlight search was a control.)

31 **(a)** (i)

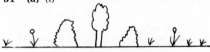

grasses, flowering herbs, shrubs, small trees

(ii)

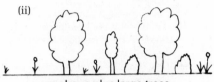

as above plus large trees.

(b) Succession **(c)** Increase
(d) Climax community
(e) Lack of light

32 **(a)** Migratory animals breed in one area and spend the rest of the year elsewhere.
(b) The insects which they feed on would be dead.
(c) Each feeds at a different height.
(d) Swallows return first, when the air is cold and insects are not carried up very high. As the air warms up later on, the insects are carried high enough for house martins, and, finally, high enough for swifts.
(e) Insects are near the ground, which means that the air is becoming cold and damp.

33 **(a)** 30 organisms in 10 samples of 0.2 m² = 30 in 2 m³
= 15 in 1 m³
i.e. 15 organisms per m³
(b) 15 × 20 m³ = 300 organisms
(c) Divide the pond surface up into a grid of 100 squares and select the 10 squares in which to sample by some random method, e.g. picking numbers out of a hat.

34 **(a)** (i) 20 ÷ 10 = 2 plants per 0.25 m² quadrat
2 × 4 = 8 plants per m² of pond area
(ii) 8 × 20 = 160 horsetails in total

(b) 160 plants will be found in 20% of the pond area i.e. 160 plants in

$$\frac{20}{100} \times 20 = 4\,\text{m}^2$$

160 horsetails in 4 m² so 40 horsetails per m² in the horsetail zone

35 (a) To make sure all the eggs had been laid.

(b) 215

(c) Graph

(d) More aphids because of larger leaf area; as the branch gets thicker, there are more sites for egg laying.

(e) Destroyed by parasites; disease; effect of poor weather; eaten by predators

36	D	**37**	E	**38**	C	**39**	D
40	A	**41**	E	**42**	B	**43**	E
44	D	**45**	A	**46**	C	**47**	B

48 (a) 10 **(b)** 2 **(c)** 18

(d) Crabs

(e) Atlantic/IV and II; Pacific/I

(f) All

(g) Had to travel further to find fish

(h) Whales

49 (a) (i) Declining numbers places them in danger of extinction.
(ii) The rats might be eating puffin eggs.
(iii) Oil pollution at sea/over fishing reducing puffins' food/ disturbance of nesting sites

(b) (i) Poisoning rats may mean more chicks survive.
(ii) The increased number of cormorants means they have to look for new sources of food.
(iii) Cormorants are a protected species.

(c) (i) 200 birds × 5 salmon per day × 30 days = 30 000 salmon
(ii) They are a pest for the managers of the salmon river because they are eating the product, i.e. the young salmon.

50 (a) Indians hunted them with bows and arrows, so more buffalo escaped.

(b) 1870–1880

(c) Building of the Union Pacific Railway/professional hunters

(d) $2\frac{1}{2} \times 6 = 15$ million animals

(e) He killed lots of buffalo.

(f) Buffalo skins could be sold for money.

(g) Removed their source of food, clothing, etc. so many Indians starved.

(h) 1906

51 (a) starfish, worms, small fish, brant goose

(b) Change in the temperature and salinity of water.

(c) Mould

(d) Lack of food caused by a break in the food chain

(e) Stabilised the shore and protected it from erosion

(f) Mould

52 (a) Reduced the area inhabited by natural shrubs and therefore reduced their number

(b) Very sparce, due to lack of light

(c) Reduce the number and diversity of animals by reducing their food and habitats

(d) It is a plant growing in the wrong place, to the detriment of the natural species.

(e) Cut them down and dig them out.

(f) In some cases, new species can be useful, e.g. food plants like potato.

53 (a) 5%

(b) Cheaper, poorer quality land, not used by farmers

(c) Colder climate on poor soil

(d) Monoculture damages the natural species.

(e) More stable/more protection for animals/more plant species at the bottom part of the hedge, which is wider.

(f) Allows seeds to be available as food for animals during the winter months.

(g) Allows hedges to establish themselves/less disturbance to wildlife/there are always some seeds available

(h) Increases the number of trees

(i) Allows wild plants to grow naturally without competition from cultivated plants

54 (a) Sewage fungus
(b) Blanket weed, bacteria, annelids and midge larvae
(c) Annelids and midge larvae
(d) Suspended solids block out the light, therefore no photo-synthesis
(e) Trout
(f) Disappears completely at first
(g) Trout

55 B **56** D **57** E **58** A

59 **1** Salmonella; **2** Escherichia;
3 diplococci; **4** Streptococcus;
5 cocci; **6** Spirilla; **7** Vibrio

60 (a) In the lower bend of the flask's neck.
(b) Bacteria will get in.
(c) Heat, water, food
(d) (i) T (ii) M and S (iii) S
(iv) Larger opening to the air so more bacteria can get in.

61 (a) Rubbish, rotting food, soil, dirt, etc.
(b) Should be covered so that flies cannot reach it.
(c) Culturing
(d) Keep culture plates closed after innoculation; incubate at 25 °C; wash hands before and after experiments; report any spills to the teacher.

62 (a) S, T, U and V
(b) 0.1% (c) T
(d) Bacteria grow faster at 25 °C than at 10 °C.
(e) Would stay clear/would become turbid after 14 days/would stay clear longer
(f) Stay clear
(g) Carbolic acid
(h) Nothing to feed on

63 (a) 3 line graphs on the same axes
(b) Bacterial reproduction
(c) Discs more uniform than leaves
(d) To prevent contamination
(e) Decomposition/decay
(f) Secrete digestive enzymes and then absorb products of the digestion
(g) X decomposes more easily; started with more bacteria in X
(h) Mesh bag/hedge/ground/air/leaves.
(i) Sterilise bags/leave bags in sterile environment/rinse bags at start in sterilised water

64 D **65** E **66** A **67** B

68 (a) Produce poisonous substances, called toxins
(b) Causes surroundings to be too acidic for bacteria to grow
(c) Both involve dehydration
(d) Temperature of the deep freeze stops bacterial growth, fridge just slows it down.
(e) Canning

69 (a) S (b) Contained sugar
(c) 35 °C (d) CO_2
(e) Too cold

70 (a) Bacteria
(b) They are in the milk inside the cow.
(c) Sterilised milk with no bacteria would stay fresh; pasteurised milk with some bacteria would be relatively fresh; untreated milk with lots of bacteria would be sour.
(d) Temperatures too low for the sterilised and pasteurised milks or not enough time at correct temperature or caps left off at the beginning, allowing bacteria to enter.
(e) (i) CO_2 (ii) Respiration
(iii) Gives them energy from food (iv) Heat
(f) (i) Milk (ii) Excretion

71 **1** Meat cooked until brown on outside only—could still be uncooked in middle, and therefore contain bacteria.
2 Cooked meat carried on same board as uncooked meat—cooked meat could become recontaminated.
3 Left in warm kitchen—bacteria could continue to grow in warmth.
4 Meat rewarmed—bacteria still not killed.

72 (a) Heats up fridge
(b) (i) Boiling in water; using a sterilising solution
(ii) So there are no bacteria in the water which could harm the baby when it is used to make up the milk
(c) So that the milk is cooled down quickly to prevent bacterial growth.
(d) The baby care manual, because young babies need to be protected

73 **(a)** Too costly/food is too bulky—would need very large refrigerators

(b) Lowering pH. Pickling

(c) Dehydration. Raisins, etc.

(d) To keep out air, which would allow the grass to rot

(e) It is dependent on a spell of dry, sunny weather.

74 E **75** A **76** B **77** B

78 D **79** C **80** B **81** D

82 E

83 **(a)** M = 0 mm; R = 4 mm; S = 6 mm; T = 0 mm

(b) T **(c)** M

(d) M = 0 mm; R = 9 mm; S = 8 mm; T = 3 mm

(e) S

(f) It has the best combined effect on both bacteria.

84 **(a)** 2 **(b)** Man

(c) Carries the disease from one person to another

(d) No

(e) In the blood the mosquito takes from an infected person.

(f) Mouth parts

(g) Salivary glands

(h) Passed into the person's blood when the mosquito 'spits' saliva down its mouthparts when feeding.

85 **(a)** Prevents them getting oxygen

(b) Mosquitos can't develop a resistance to this method.

(c) British mosquitos would then be able to carry the disease to other people.

(d) Eastern Mediterranean

(e) Europe, Americas

(f) Increase in human population

86 **(a)** From the mother

(b) Had the disease when young therefore she could have natural immunity

(c) Vaccination

(d) Before the girl is old enough to become pregnant

(e) Can't bring the disease into the home

87 **(a)** W

(b) Most people died round this pump.

(c) Drinking contaminated water

(d) Shut down the pump/boil the water

(e) Bad sanitation

(f) Overcrowding/no medicine/poor hygiene

88 **(a)** 1796–1977 = 181 years

(b) West Africa

(c) Afghanistan

(d) Body develops antibodies. These remain in the body and provide protection.

(e) In case it ever appears again.

89 **(a)** Vaccination, early diagnosis, antibiotics, better housing

(b) See if they all had the same milk source.

(c) Pasteurisation/heat treatment

(d) Heat milk to 63 °C, keep at this temperature for 30 minutes then cool rapidly.

or Heat milk to 70 °C, keep at this temperature for 15 seconds then cool rapidly.

90 **(a)** To protect them while in quarantine from other imported animals which might be infected.

(b) To ensure that they are free of the disease before they come into contact with the general public.

(c) The disease can appear any time up until six months after the animal has been infected.

(d) Wild animals could cross the borders, carrying the disease.

(e) They are all islands.

Theme 3
Maintenance and Organisation

1 B **2** D **3** A **4** C
5 C
6 (a) K coarse focus; L fine focus;
M eyepiece; N nosepiece;
O objective; P stage
(b) × 400
(c) X low power; Z medium power;
Y high power
(d) 2 mm
7 (a) × 500
(b) × 2500
(c) Centriole, nucleus, nucleolus,
cell membrane, cytoplasm
(d) Pores in nuclear membrane;
nucleolus has three light spots
in it; size of nucleus
(e) Mitochondrion, Golgi body,
microvilli, rough endoplasmic
reticulum, pinocytic vesicle
(f) Rough endoplasmic reticulum
(g) Microvilli, pinocytic vesicle
(h) Increase surface area for
absorption
(i) Golgi body
8 (a) K cell wall; L cytoplasm;
M vacuole; N nucleus
(b) Y and Z
(c) No chloroplasts
(d) Y
(e) Spiral chloroplast in Z; nucleus
in centre of cell in Z
9 (a) M, N and P
(b) K, L and O
(c) K nerve cell; L Amoeba;
N epidermal cells
10 (a) Protection
(b) Chloroplasts
(c) Photosynthesis—leaf
(d) K (e) Support
(f) Long with pointed ends, thick
walls
(g) Transport of water
(h) Support
(i) Hollow tubes—transport water;
thick walls—give support
(j) To allow absorption of water
11 C **12** E **13** D **14** B
15 A **16** E **17** B
18 (a) e.g. amylase: substrate starch,
product maltose
(b) e.g. photosynthesis, respiration

(c) Temperature, pH, concentration
of substrate, concentration of
enzyme
(d) The enzyme's activity would
cease. Heat destroys the enzyme.
19 (a) Graph
(b) Too cold for enzyme activity
(c) Enzyme has been destroyed by
heat.
(d) (i) 35 °C (ii) 74
(e) (i) 50 (ii) 38
20 (a) Brown/reddish brown
(b) To get rid of food particles
(c) To promote production of saliva
(d) To allow mixing to take place
(e) There was a lot of starch present
when the drops were first
added.
(f) Less starch present
(g) No starch present
(h) Test the remaining solution in
the syringe with Benedict's
solution.
21 (a) Graph (b) 35 °C
(c) Decreases rate (d) 30 °C
(e) Decreases rate (f) N
(g) No activity recorded for this
enzyme at this temperature.
(h) Read from graph
(i) M, because the optimum
temperature is higher.
22 (a) Protein (b) 1 cm³ (c) 1 cm³
(d) Must be the same in each tube
(e) M
(f) This tube provides the correct
pH, and the enzyme has not
been boiled.
(g) To show that it was the enzyme
which was breaking down the
egg white.
(h) (i) 37 °C–40 °C
(ii) This is body temperature/
optimum temperature.
23 (a) Act on specific substrates; most
efficient at an optimum
temperature; needed in very
small quantities; speed up the
rate of a reaction; affected by
extremes of pH (4 only)
(b) The stains contain organic
compounds.

(c) 37 °C

(d) Enzymes are denatured (destroyed) at high temperatures and cannot function.

(e) Use cooler water, therefore less energy required to heat it.

24 E   25 D   26 B   27 A

28 D   29 C

30 (a) Sugars; amino acids

(b) Water molecules move into the cell.

(c) Concentration of cell sap of X becomes more dilute than Y.

(d) Water will move from X to Y.

(e) Water molecules would move outwards.

(f) The high salt content means that the roots will have difficulty in absorbing water.

31 (a) Increased by 7 cm³

(b) Water molecules moved inwards by osmosis.

(c) Decreased by 6 cm³

(d) Water molecules moved outwards by osmosis.

(e) It would increase in volume, because water would be taken in by osmosis.

(f) To allow the egg to expand and contract; egg shell is waterproof

32 (a) The pores are very small so the smaller water molecules can move through easily. Larger sugar molecules cannot.

(b) Cell membranes

(c) To remove the excess sugar from the surface.

(d) To remove excess water.

(e) 2.2 g

(f) $\dfrac{2.2}{13.1} \times 100 = 16.8\%$

(g) Water has passed from a region of low solute concentration to a region of high solute concentration, hence the sausage swells up.

(h) Sausage no longer bends.

(i) Turgid

33 (a) Osmosis   (b) Loss of water

(c) Wilted   (d) Turgid   (e) Wilt

(f) Lose water by osmosis

34 (a) Turgidity of cells

(b) So that the turgid cells are not crushed

(c) So that they are fully turgid

(d) Transpiration rate is greatly reduced at night time, therefore there is less risk of wilting.

35 (a) N   (b) M and L

(c) Blood cells; plasma proteins

(d) Ultrafiltration

(e) K and L

(f) Carries urine to the pelvis of the kidney

36 (a) Amino acids   (b) Glucose

(c) Reabsorbed into the blood

(d) Liquid in the collecting duct

(e) Blood pressure

37 (a) (i) Decreases   (ii) Increases

(b) (i) K and L; M and N
    (ii) L and M; N and O

(c) Osmosis

(d) Contractile vacuole

(e) (i) Coming in   (ii) Going out

38 (a) Reptiles, birds, mammals

(b) Mammals

(c) Reptiles and birds

(d) Freshwater fish and frog

(e) Largest Bowman's capsule

(f) Long loops of Henlé

(g) Need to lose a lot of water in their urine

39 E   40 A   41 A   42 D

43 B   44 C   45 B   46 D

47 C

48 (a) 1 flower;   2 fruit;   3 leaf;
    4 bud;   5 stem;
    6 lateral root;   7 tap root;

(b) (i) 6   (ii) 4   (iii) 3, 5, 7   (iv) 1
    (v) 2   (vi) 3   (vii) 5

49 (a) K epidermis; L cortex; M phloem; N xylem; O pith

(b) Food transport

(c) Water transport

(d) Vascular bundles

(e) Parenchyma/packing tissue

(f) Dicotyledon, because of the circular arrangement of the vascular bundles.

50 (a) M epidermis/piliferous layer; R cortex; S xylem; T phloem; U root hair

(b) (i) U   (ii) R   (iii) T   (iv) S
    (v) M

(c) Tissue   (d) Organ

(e) Organ system

51 (a) O   (b) N   (c) P   (d) P

(e) O   (f) P   (g) P   (h) Q

(i) M

172

52 **(a)** (i) By placing it in boiling water.
(ii) To allow iodine to enter the cells more readily/to allow chlorophyll to come out.
(b) (i) By placing in boiling alcohol.
(ii) To allow colour change with iodine to be seen easily.
(c) To see if chlorophyll is necessary for starch production.
(d) No starch present. No CO_2 would be absorbed because stomata are sealed with Vaseline.

53 **(a)** Oxygen
(b) Test it with a glowing splint. Splint should re-light.
(c) Graph
(d) To allow the apparatus and plant to stabilise at the new temperature.
(e) 25 °C
(f) 46 bubbles
(g) Amount of CO_2 present; amount of light

54 **(a)** More chlorophyll present
(b) Above 25% light intensity, the leaves cannot photosynthesise any quicker.
(c) More photosynthesis, therefore faster growth.
(d) By food substances transported from other green leaves.
(e) Not as much stored food in variegated species.

55 **(a)** Variegated
(b) To remove any starch already there
(c) To make sure plenty of starch is present
(d) Indicates photosynthesis has taken place
(e) Kill the leaf in boiling water, decolourise it in boiling alcohol, wash it in cold water and add iodine solution.

(f)

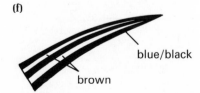

blue/black

brown

56 **(a)** Y
(b) Labelling, equal amounts of BI solution in each tube, discs cut from the same leaf, all conditions apart from light the same.
(c) Y   **(d)** C
(e) A—B/I solution would go purple;
B—B/I solution would go yellow;
C—B/I solution would remain orange
(f) A—photosynthesis is taking place and using up the CO_2;
B—respiration is taking place and producing CO_2; C—no plant present to change the atmosphere

57 **(a)** To absorb CO_2
(b) To act as a control for the pellets
(c) To make the apparatus airtight
(d) Stomata are mainly on the lower surface of leaves.
(e) Iodine solution
(f) Killed in boiling water, decolourised in boiling alcohol
(g)

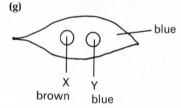

X   Y
brown   blue

blue

(h) CO_2 is necessary for the production of starch in leaves.
(i) The leaf should be kept in the dark for several hours to de-starch it.

58 B   **59** C   **60** D   **61** A
62 C   **63** A   **64** E
65 Food should be in **liquid form** or ground up with water. **Equal amounts** of Benedict's solution and food should be used. The tube should be placed in a **boiling water bath**. The tube should remain in the bath for **two minutes**. A **red/brown precipitate** indicates the presence of reducing sugar.
66 **(a)** K   **(b)** R   **(c)** N   **(d)** L
(e) S   **(f)** O   **(g)** Q
(h) U, P, S   **(i)** P, S   **(j)** T

67 (a) Very little space for storage/
little digestion actually occurs.

(b) 4 hours

(c) Digestion and absorption

(d) Large intestine

(e) Extraction of water and storage
prior to defaecation

68 (a) B **(b)** A **(c)** B **(d)** D

(e) E

69 (a) Allows some materials through
and not others

(b) Smooth internal surface: surface
area not increased internally by
villi.

(c) Reducing sugar would be
present, starch would not be
present.

(d) Some starch is broken down
into sugar, which can diffuse
through the Visking tubing.
(Undigested starch is too large
to pass through the tubing.)

70 (a) Chocolate dessert, because it
contains most energy and
protein for the same cost.

(b) Protein is vital for the growth
of the baby.

(c) Chocolate dessert

(d) Apple dessert

(e) Vitamins and minerals

71 (a) Water

(b) Mineral salts, vitamins

(c) Cornflakes: $\dfrac{20 \times 90}{100} = 18\,\text{g}$

(d) Milk: $\dfrac{40 \times 7}{100} = 2.8\,\text{g}$

(e) Milk: $\dfrac{40 \times 280}{100} = 112\,\text{kJ}$

Cornflakes: $\dfrac{20 \times 1500}{100} = 300\,\text{kJ}$

Yoghurt: $\dfrac{25 \times 1400}{100} = 350\,\text{kJ}$

Sugar: $\dfrac{5 \times 1600}{100} = 80\,\text{kJ}$

Coffee: $\dfrac{50 \times 80}{100} = 40\,\text{kJ}$

Total $= 882\,\text{kJ}$

72 (a) Scurvy

(b) Deficiency in vitamin C

(c) These juices are rich in vitamin
C.

(d) e.g. oranges

(e) Boiling destroys the vitamin C.

(f) Give vitamin C solution
intravenously (by-passes oral
consumption).

73 (a) Weak bones, bandy legs

(b) Sunlight contains ultra-violet
light which is essential for the
manufacture of vitamin D.

(d) Breast-fed infants receive no
vitamin D in their mother's milk.
Bottle-fed children gain vitamin
D from their milk.

(e) Nothing present in diet to
remedy the vitamin D deficiency.

(f) Exposing more skin to sunlight;
bottle feeding; cod liver oil
supplement

74 (a) Carries glucose from the ileum,
and the amount of sugar here
depends on when the last meal
was taken.

(b) Contains the breakdown
products of haemoglobin

(c) Protein in diet

(d) Hepatic portal vein

(e) Carried in the blood to the
kidneys and excreted

(f) A and D are fat-soluble vitamins
which are stored in the liver.

(g) Hepatic artery

(h) Storage of bile

75 E **76** A **77** D **78** C

79 C

80 (a) Water, mineral salts

(b) Sugar **(c)** X

(d) Arrangement of vascular tissue

(e) Xylem

(f)

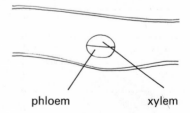

phloem   xylem

(g) Veins

81 **(a)** Z
   (b) Light intensity increases transpiration rate.
   (c) Humidity; temperature
   (d) Any suitable experiment
   (e) X

82 **(a)** No oil on roots; no water on outside of container; all leaves outside the flask
   (b) Place on balance and record weight loss.
   (c) Any suitable experiment, e.g. fan, bright light.
   (d) Answer depends on experiment in **(c)**.
   (e) Put dye in water. Cut sections of plant and see where dye is found.

83 **(a)** See Table A2 below.
   (b) The water content of each item would vary.
   (c) Greater in plants.
   (d) (i) N (ii) Mg (iii) P

84 **(a)** Phloem is a living tissue and so is destroyed by high temperatures.
   (b) Doesn't do any mechanical damage, i.e. doesn't harm the xylem.
   (c) CO_2 used in photosynthesis to make carbohydrates. These are transported in phloem out of the leaves.
   (d) (i) Can be moved upwards and downwards
        (ii) In phloem

85 **(a)** Contain starch, not sugar
   (b) Sugar is being transported in phloem.
   (c) Roots store starch.

	Order of abundance most——→least				
Soil	Ca	Mg	K	N	P
Knapweed	Ca	N	K	Mg	P
Birdsfoot trefoil	Ca	N	K	Mg	P
Salad burnet	Ca	N	K	Mg	P
Sedge	N	K	Ca	Mg	P

Table A2

(d) No photosynthesis. All carbohydrates transported away.
(e) Photosynthesis has occurred, therefore carbohydrates are present.

86 B 87 E 88 C 89 C
90 D 91 E 92 E
93 **(a)** C and B **(b)** A and B **(c)** B
   (d) Oxygenated and deoxygenated blood kept separate
   (e) Lungs, organs and tissues of the body
   (f) Lungs, tissues
   (g) Carbon dioxide **(h)** Urea
   (i) Blood passes through the heart twice in every circuit of the body.

94 **(a)** 1, 3, 4, 5, 10
   (b) Atria **(c)** 2, 6, 7, 8, 9
   (d) Liver **(e)** Left
   (f) Vein carrying oxygenated blood
   (g) (i) R to Q (ii) Y to X
   (h) (i) deoxygenated;
        (ii) oxygenated;
        (iii) deoxygenated

95 **(a)**

Girls		Boys	
Mary	72	John	70
Martha	74	James	70
Annabel	76	Timothy	68
Rachel	78	Matthew	70
Jane	72	Ivan	71
Joan	78	Alan	69
Clare	76	Ian	70
Anne	74	Frank	72

   (b) 75 **(c)** 70
   (d) Girls
   (e) Martha—up 52
   (f) Ivan—up 41
   (g) Increases circulation of blood to body, and therefore more oxygen available for respiration to provide energy

96 **(a)** Red blood cells have a life span of approximately 100 days.
(b) Short bones of the body/bone marrow
(c) To carry oxygen
(d) Broken down in the liver. Some products of the breakdown are recycled, others are excreted.
(e) Shape; size; lack of nucleus in red blood corpuscles
(f) Red blood cells are not just found in veins. Also, they perform a useful function.

97 **(a)** R and Q   **(b)** T and M
(c) U, V, W   **(d)** Right
(e) Lungs lie close to the heart.
(f) Left   **(g)** Left
(h) Needs to pump blood further
(i) (i) open   (ii) closed
(j) W
(k) Blood passes through vessel M into the left atrium. It passes through the bicuspid valve into the left ventricle. When the left atrium contracts, the rest of the blood is forced into the left ventricle. When the left ventricle contracts, the bicuspid valve closes and the blood is forced into the aorta (vessel N).

98 **(a)** Oxygen, glucose, amino acids
(b) Distances involved are too great for diffusion to be effective.
(c) Increase
(d) Death, due to lack of oxygen
(e) Lack of oxygen, lack of food, build up of CO_2 and other wastes.

99 **(a)** False   **(b)** True
(c) False   **(d)** True   **(e)** True

100 **(a)** $2.2 \, N/cm^2$ **(b)** $0.8 \, N/cm^2$
(c) 120   **(d)** B–C
(e) B   **(f)** C

101 **(a)** Veins
(b) Blood has been forced forwards by the finger, but the vein does not fill up because the valve prevents backflow.
(c) Vein would fill up and become visible.
(d) Blood flows in one direction only in veins.

(e) Water molecules pass from soil water into the cell sap of root hairs by osmosis.
(f) Very high pressure
(g) Transpiration stream
(h) Animals have a pump (i.e. heart); plants have no such pump. Also, circulation is unidirectional in animals.

102 B	**103** C	**104** B	**105** D
106 B	**107** B	**108** E	**109** D
110 E	**111** A	**112** D	

113 **(a)** Histogram
(b) Exercise requires energy. Energy is released from food by respiration. Oxygen is required for aerobic respiration.
(c) $29 - 10 = 19$

% increase $\dfrac{19}{10} \times 100 = 190\%$

(d) No
(e) No information about the speed of the individuals.

114 **(a)** Oxygen diffuses into the blood.
(b) Carbon dioxide diffuses into the alveoli.
(c) No net diffusion in either direction.
(d) Haemoglobin
(e) Cells are using up oxygen faster than normal breathing can supply it, therefore breathing rate must increase.
(f) Could not carry oxygen due to formation of stable compound, carboxyhaemoglobin.
(g) Faster heartbeat/breathing rate
(h) Red blood cells can no longer carry oxygen.
(i) More red blood cells per unit volume
(j) S/he will have more red blood cells per unit volume, therefore the oxygen supply to the muscles will be increased.

115 **(a)** W—orange; X—red; Y—yellow
(b) Plant uses up CO_2 so its concentration decreases.
(c) W
(d) Respiration
(e) Respiration and photosynthesis balance.

116 (a) Supported by external atmospheric pressure
(b) Soak them and warm them to encourage germination.
(c) Liquid paraffin maintains anaerobic conditions.
(d) Mercury and its vapours are poisonous.
(e) CO_2
(f) Seeds respired anaerobically.

117 (a) 12.5 **(b)** 0.5 **(c)** 25
(d) 7 years **(e)** Never

118 (a) (i) Trachea (ii) Lungs
(iii) Rib cage (iv) Diaphragm
(b) (i) Increases (ii) Decreases
(iii) Into balloon
(iv) High pressure to low pressure
(c) (i) Increases
(ii) Air forced out of the lungs
(iii) Decreases (iv) Inhalation
(v) So that the pressure in X may increase and decrease
(vi) No, cannot breathe outside the lung
(vii) Urination/defaecation/eating/boredom

119 (a) dry 50 mm; damp 50 mm; glucose 49 mm; ATP 43 mm.
(b) (i) No change—muscle hasn't contracted
(ii) Muscle has contracted
(c) Approx 12%
(d) ATP makes energy available

120 (a) 100 m 9.5 dm³; 1500 m 17 dm³; 10 000 m 17 dm³
(b) Inversely proportional
(c) Proportional
(d) 17 dm³
(e) 10 000 m race has same oxygen debt as 1500 m.
(f) Anaerobic

121 E **122** B

123 (a) Positively phototropic
(b) So that they are equally stimulated on all sides and grow straight
(c) Contain more auxin because it is not destroyed by the light.
(d) (i) Equal amounts on all sides
(ii) More on the left side
(iii) More growth on the

left-hand side than on the right.
(iv) Light destroys auxin. Therefore, the side nearest the the light has less auxin. The side furthest from the light consequently grows more quickly, so the plant bends towards the light.

124 (a) X **(b)** Y, Z
(c) Bud—keeps it protected from the rain
Flower—allows insect pollination
(d) Negatively geotropic and positively-phototropic. Long upright stem carries capsule above surrounding vegetation so that it can be shaken by wind.

125 B **126** A

127 D **128** C

129 (a) M pupil; N lens; O sclera;
P choroid; Q optic nerve;
R retina; S vitreous humour;
T ciliary muscle;
U aqueous humour; V cornea;
W conjunctiva; X iris
(b) (i) Q (ii) O, S, U (iii) X
(iv) W (v) N (vi) P (vii) O
(c) Diffusion

130 (a) Iris **(b)** Pupil
(c) I R = 6 mm; II R = 16 mm.
(d) II
(e) Radial muscles
(f) (i) Circular muscles
(ii) Radial muscles

131 (a) (i) I (ii) II
(b) X suspensory ligaments;
Y ciliary muscles
(c) Stretched **(d)** Contracted
(e) Suspensory ligaments relaxed, therefore no tension on the lens
(f) Muscle does work when it contracts

132 **(a)** False   **(b)** True   **(c)** True
  (d) False   **(e)** See Table A3 below.

Name	Description	Effect
sweating	evaporation of water from the skin	heat taken from the skin to evaporate sweat
vasodilation	blood vessels in the skin open wider; more blood at surface; skin becomes red	blood carries heat—more heat lost
vasoconstriction	blood vessels in skin narrowed; less blood at surface; skin becomes pale	heat lost more slowly
shivering	rapid reflex contraction of muscles	contracting muscles produce heat

Table A3

133 **(a)** In food
  (b) Respiration in cells
  (c) Its temperature would fall and it would eventually die.
  (d) Evaporation of water from the tongue takes heat from the body.
  (e) They are so small that they lose heat very quickly.
  (f) It reduces their heat loss and enables them to survive until they can feed again.

134 A   **135** C   **136** E   **137** D

138 **(a)**

	Condition			
	I	II	III	IV
Start	1	2	0	2
2	1	2	1	1
4	1	2	1	1
6	1	4	0	0
8	1	3	0	1
10	0	5	0	0
Total	5	18	2	5

Table A4

(b) Woodlice are looking for suitable conditions.
  (c) (i) False   (ii) True   (iii) False (iv) False
  (d) (i) dry = 7; damp = 23
  (ii) dark = 23; light = 7
  (iii) dry/light = 2; damp/light = 5
  (iv) damp/light = 5; damp/dark = 18
  (e) Dark and damp

139 **(a)** Graph
  (b) To spread heat quickly.
  (c) To keep hottest and coldest away from each other.
  (d) 20 °C

140 **(a)** A tap or blow to the tendon beneath the knee cap
  (b) A stretch receptor in the tendon
  (c) Sensory neuron
  (d) In the grey matter of the spinal cord
  (e) Motor neuron
  (f) In the grey matter of the spinal cord
  (g) In the grey matter of the spinal cord
  (h) A muscle
  (i) A rapid spontaneous upwards jerk by the whole lower leg

141 **(a)** Reflex   **(b)** Touch   **(c)** Skin
  (d) Nervous system

(e) Knee jerk reflex

(f) Too rough/this reflex has not yet developed

142 B   **143** D   **144** C   **145** E

146 (a) M radius; R ulna; S humerus; T biceps/flexor; W triceps/extensor

(b) To attach muscle to bone

(c) To attach bone to bone

(d) Lubricates the joint

(e) Joints have to be able to move therefore ligaments must stretch

(f) If tendons were elastic then they would stretch when muscles contracted, and the bones wouldn't move.

147 (a) Upper thigh muscle

(b) Lower thigh muscle

(c) Antagonistic

(d) Calf muscle

(e) Shin muscle

(f) Upper thigh muscle; calf muscle

(g) Lifts the whole weight of the body.

(h) Couldn't flex the ankle.

148 (a) X ball and socket; Y hinge; Z hinge

(b) R support, protection of spinal cord; S breathing, protection of lungs and heart; T support, movement

(c) Long neck

149 (a) Vertebra   **(b)** Rib   **(c)** Hinge

(d) Protection of lungs; attachment of muscles

(e) Intercostal muscles

(f) Move rib cage during breathing

(g) Sternum

150 (a) One bone in upper part of limb; two bones in lower part of limb

(b) Longer fingers

(c) Flying   **(d)** Bird

(e) Fewer carpels

(f) Five-fingered

(g) Crocodile, man, bat, seal

151 C   **152** D   **153** A   **154** E

155 (a) Deficiency of insulin

(b) People over forty   **(c)** No

(d) (i) Less than one year
(ii) Less than 10 years

(e) Insulin injections

(f) Sugar in urine; ketones in blood and urine

(g) Require sugar when food intake is delayed or when vigorous exercise is taken.

156 (a) Fatty acids; blood sugar or fats; carbohydrates

(b) Hormones

(c) Increases them by converting glycogen into glucose

(d) Exercise, fright

(e) Converts it into fat or energy

(f) Increase

(g) Diabetes

(h) Diet correction; insulin injections

Theme 4
Development and Continuity of Life

1 A   **2** E   **3** B   **4** D

5 C   **6** E

7 (a) (i) 2
(ii) Same as parent (diploid)

(b) (i) 4   (ii) $\frac{1}{2}$ the parent's number (haploid)

8 (a) (i) Tip, buds, developing leaves
(ii) Tip of main root, tip of lateral roots
(iii) Growth/increase in size
(iv) Anthers and ovary/ovule
(v) Production of gametes

(b) (i) Skin, lining of gut
(ii) Replacement and repair
(iii) Growth

(iv) Reproductive organs, i.e. testes, ovaries
(v) Gamete production

9 E   **10** B   **11** C

12 (a) X-rays can cause cancer or mutations.

(b) Young children

(c) Growing tissue

(d) Carcinogen

13 (a) (i) A tumour in which the cancer cells invade surrounding healthy tissue
(ii) Slow-growing masses of cells which are not invasive

(b) A substance which can cause cancer: X-rays, UV light, radiation, mustard gas

(c) (i) Treatment of cancer using X-rays and other radiation. Cancer cells are more susceptible to low radiation than normal cells.
(ii) Treatment of cancer by the administration of drugs which kill cancer cells and do not damage normal cells.

(d) (i) May damage healthy cells
(ii) Sickness and vomiting

(e) Checking people at risk to see if they have cancer.

14 A   **15** D   **16** C   **17** E

18 B

19 **(a)** S anther; T pollen grain; U filament; V nectary; W stigma; X style; Y ovary; Z ovule

(b) S, T, U

(c) W, X, Y, Z

(d) Z

(e) Nectaries

20 **(a)** Petal   **(b)** Anthers
(c) Nectar   **(d)** Stigma
(e) Ovary   **(f)** Filament
(g) Sepals   **(h)** Style   **(i)** Ovule
(j) Stamen

21 **(a)** Runners   **(b)** Asexual
(c) Produced laterally by parent plant. They produce adventitious roots and shoots at a node; this develops into a new plant.

(d) Can produce lots of runners

(e) Spread so quickly, they leave no space. They compete for light/nutrients with other plants.

(f) (i) Sexual
(ii) Seeds are carried away and they germinate elsewhere.

22 **(a)** F pollen grain; G pollen tube; H stigma; I style; J ovary; K ovule; M filament; N sepal; O stem

(b) Carpel

(c) Pollination   **(d)** Fertilisation

(e) Pollen tube grows up to ovule, male nucleus fuses with nucleus of ovule to form zygote

(f) (i) 7
(ii) This is the number of pollen grains.
(iii) K   (iv) J
(v) Different number of ovules/ different number of pollen grains

23 **(a)** Strawberry, buttercup
(b) Plum   **(c)** Apple, rose
(d) Strawberry, buttercup
(e) Strawberry has larger petals, fewer ovaries, fewer stamens, larger sepals.
(f) P strawberry; Q rose; R apple; S buttercup; T plum

24 B   **25** A   **26** E   **27** C

28 D

29 See Table A5 below.

Characteristic	Egg	Sperm	Both
Cell membrane			✓
Tail		✓	
Dies if not fertilised	✓	✓	
Large food store	✓		
Females	✓		
Swims		✓	
Males		✓	

Table A5

	Example	No. of eggs	Size of egg	Food supply for embryo	Oxygen supply for embryo
Mammal	Mouse	Few	Microscopic	From the mother	From the mother
Fish	Pike	Very numerous	Small	Inside the egg	Outside the egg
Bird	Chicken	Few	Large	Inside the egg	Outside the egg
Amphibian	Frog	Numerous	Medium	Inside the egg	Outside the egg

Table A6

31 (a) U Cowper's/prostate gland;
V ureter; W penis;
X vas deferens (sperm tube);
Y testis
(b) Y (c) X (d) U (e) W
(f) Become erect (g) Vagina
(h) Vasectomy—permanent;
condom—temporary

32 (a) P ovary; Q oviduct; R uterus;
S vagina; T vulva; U vagina;
V oviduct; W ovary; X uterus;
Y vulva
(b) I P; II W
(c) I R; II X
(d) I Q; II V
(e) Position of ovary; human has
one uterus, but rat has two
(f) S
(g) Permanent—sterilisation;
temporary—intra-uterine device
(IUD), cap, pill

33 E **34** B **35** B **36** D

37 (a) $\dfrac{12}{20} \times 100 = 60\%$

(b) $\dfrac{20}{20} \times 100 = 100\%$.

(c) Removal of the seed coat allows
water to enter the seed quickly
and initiates the process of
germination.

(d) It prevents the entry of water
into the seed and prevents
premature germination.

(e) That removal of the seed coat
has no effect on the rate of
germination (null hypothesis);
or increases the rate of
germination.

38 See Table A7 below.

Fruit	Dispersal	Special adaptation
U (dandelion)	Wind	Hairs
X (elm)	Wind	Wing
Z (gorse)	Self	Pod splits open
V (poppy)	Wind	Seeds in capsule
Y (blackberry)	Animal	Seeds eaten and passed through animal in faeces
W (burdock)	Animal	Hooks catch in animals' fur

Table A7

39 (a) Dish A: $\frac{6}{10} = 60\%$;

Dish B: $\frac{43}{100} = 43\%$

(b) A suitable temperature, and the presence of oxygen.

(c) Higher rate of germination in dish A because there were fewer seeds competing for the same space and water, so proportionally each seed in dish A had more resources than those in dish B.

(d) There was more water for cell growth and expansion, and more space compared to dish B.

(e) In dish B the lack of resources may have stopped growth in some seeds and made them more vulnerable to fungal attack, **or** more seeds used means a higher chance of introducing contaminated individuals.

40 (a) Water dispersal—they float

(b) To allow them to float

(c) To keep out sea water during dispersal

(d) They are carried in sea currents (probably the Gulf Stream).

(e) Water, suitable temperature, oxygen

(f) Too cold

41 (a) J leaf; K stem; L cotyledons; M hypocotyl; N root

(b) Epigeal—cotyledons above the ground

(c) Both green/both photosynthesise

(d) Dicotyledonous. Two cotyledons

(e) Bird may have eaten holly berries, passing seed out in faeces.

42 1 H; 2 E; 3 D; 4 F; 5 C; 6 G; 7 B; 8 A

43 (a) I, II **(b)** I

(c) Flowers are produced before the leaves

(d) IV

(e) No flowers are produced

(f) VI

(g) Flowers are produced early in the year.

(h) V

44 A **45** E **46** D **47** E

48 See Table A8 below.

(b) $68 \div 0.12 = 567$

(c) Eye of 7 day chick is 6 times larger.

49 (a) M placenta; N umbilical cord; O amniotic fluid; P embryo/baby; Q amnion

(b) Provides food/provides oxygen/takes away carbon dioxide and other waste products.

(c) (i) takes food/oxygen to baby
(ii) prevents damage
(iii) holds amniotic fluid

(d) Mother's blood pressure is too high—would damage embryo.

50 (a) The time between conception and birth

(b) Mammals

(c) (i) The larger the body size, the longer the gestation period.
(ii) Blue whale

Diagram	Name	Length/mm	Actual size/mm
W	egg	34	68
X	sperm	30	0.12
Y	head of $3\frac{1}{2}$ day chick	20	4
Y	eye of $3\frac{1}{2}$ day chick	5	1
Z	head of 7 day chick	25	12.5
Z	eye of 7 day chick	12	6

Table A8

51 **(a)** (i) Graph
(ii) 0 months (birth)
(iii) Yes, the table gives the *average* weights and it is possible to find a girl of above average weight, or a boy of below average weight.
(b) (i) 10 years
(ii) 11–14 years
(iii) Developing faster; earlier onset of puberty
(iv) Development of body hair; development of breasts; beginning of menstruation; broadening of hips

52 D   **53** C   **54** A   **55** B

56 E

57 **(a)** Tall
(b) Homozygous
(c) Tt (heterozygous)
(d) Homozygous tall, heterozygous tall, homozygous short
(e) Alleles

58 **(a)** Transfer of pollen from the anther to the stigma of the same plant
(b) Enclose the flowers in a polythene bag.
(c) 42   **(d)** 14   **(e)** 7   **(f)** 3:1
(g) The original 8 round seeds were heterozygous Rr, where R = round and r = wrinkled.

	R	r
R	RR	Rr
r	Rr	rr

3:1

(h) Pod U contains 8 round peas only. These could be RR or Rr. Allow them to grow and self-pollinate again. If Rr, they will yield round and wrinkled seeds. If RR, they will yield round seeds only.

59 **(a)** Short haired, because this characteristic is found in all the offspring of the cross.
(b) Heterozygous, i.e. Ss
(c) Cross them with long haired cats, i.e. do a test cross

	s	s
S	Ss	Ss
s	ss	ss

1:1

(d) 3 short-haired:1 long haired

60 **(a)** Sisters
(b) Half brother/half sister
(c) bb   **(d)** Bb
(e) The only way non-brindle pups can be produced is if she was heterozygous; her mother was non-brindle.

61 **(a)** Heterozygous
(b) This is the only way both colours of pups can be produced
(c) Homozygous black and tan
(d) Heterozygous black
(e) Homozygous black and tan
(f)

	b	b
B	Bb	Bb
b	bb	bb

1:1

62 **(a)** A and B   **(b)** AO, BO
(c) AA, AO   **(d)** BB, BO
(e) 50:50

63 **(a)** $X^{N}Y$ **(b)** $X^{n}Y$
(c) $X^{N}X^{N}$; $X^{N}X^{n}$
(d) Carrier
(e) Sex linked

64 **(a)** The striped characteristic is dominant.
(b) Horses don't carry the striped gene.
(c) Horses don't carry the striped gene.
(d)

	s	s
S	Ss	Ss
S	Ss	Ss

All foals would have stripes.

(e)

	s	s
	s	s
s	ss	ss
s	ss	ss

No foals would have stripes.

(f) To check his results

(g) Mutation

65 D   **66** E   **67** C   **68** B

69 A   **70** B

71 **(a)** Birds

(b) Camouflage

(c) Country areas

(d) Better camouflaged, therefore survived and bred

(e) Clean Air Act has brought about reduction in air pollution.

72 **(a)** Gardener's Delight

(b) Low disease resistance

(c) Spring Giant × Supercross or Gardener's Delight

(d) Ailsa Craig × Small Fry

(e) Artificial selection

73 **(a)** They know that environment doesn't affect inherited characteristics.

(b) Recessive

(c) Heterozygous

(d) $\frac{1}{4}$

(e) Father was spotted and mother was heterozygous

74 **(a)** The test group were deliberately selected to be more efficient layers.

(b) So that good layers and bad layers could mate with each other and allow mixing of genes (i.e. no selection occurring).

(c) In the hope they could pass on the genes for good egg laying to to their offspring.

(d) $212 - 202 = 10$

(e) As a comparison to ensure that it was selective breeding that caused the increase in egg laying and not some other factor.

(f) Artificial selection.